Audrey Healy

Dubliners

What's the Story?

CURRACH
PRESS

First published in 2002 by
CURRACH PRESS
55A Spruce Avenue, Stillorgan Industrial Park, Blackrock, Co Dublin

Designed by Slick Fish Design
Printed in Ireland by Betaprint, Dublin

ISBN 1 85607 900 7

Author's Acknowledgements

I would like to thank all those who assisted in the production of this book and gave permission to use photographs, texts and interviews. Thanks to Eugene McEldowney and Don Mullan for their advice and encouragement, to Thomas, Liam and Frank for proof-reading, and a special word of appreciation to Lorraine and Paul for the many hours of unpaid labour.

Thanks also to Brian Lynch of Currach Press for his help and patience on this project, and finally thanks to the many Dubliners who gave of their time and their hearts so willingly and who made this book possible.

Contents

Introduction	7
Bertie Ahern	9
Molly Allgood	12
Eamonn Andrews	14
Thomas Barnardo	16
Samuel Beckett	18
Brendan Behan	21
Willie Bermingham	23
Maeve Binchy	25
Christy Brown	27
Gabriel Byrne	29
Gay Byrne	31
Edward Carson	34
Roger Casement	36
Anthony Clare	38
Ronan Collins	41
W. T. Cosgrave	43
Shay Cullen	45
Bryan Dobson	48
Ken Doherty	50
Ronnie Drew	53
Frank Duff	56
Joe Duffy	58
Robert Emmet	60
Colin Farrell	62
Barry Fitzgerald	64
Brendan Grace	66
Tony Gregory	68
Arthur Guinness	71
Tom Hyland	73
James Joyce	75

Frank Kelly 77

Luke Kelly 79

Adrian Kennedy 81

Pat Kenny 83

Seán Lemass 86

Phil Lynott 88

Catherine McAuley 91

Molly Malone 93

Mother Mary Martin 95

Mike Murphy 97

Bryan Murray 100

Christina Noble 102

David Norris 105

Seán O'Casey 108

Maureen O'Hara 110

Charles Stewart Parnell 113

Geraldine Plunkett 115

Sarah Purser 117

George Bernard Shaw 119

Bram Stoker 122

Jonathan Swift 124

Matt Talbot 126

Arthur Wellesley 128

Marty Whelan 130

Oscar Wilde 132

Peg Woffington 134

Theobald Wolfe Tone 136

William Butler Yeats 138

Copyright acknowledgements 141

Introduction

Will the real Dubliner please step forward?

What constitutes a real Dubliner? The figure looking out over O'Connell Bridge at night? The young girl soaking up the summer sun in St Stephen's Green? The talkative taxi driver putting the world to rights? The high profile politician from his government office? The 'oul fellow holding up the bar in Dicey Reilly's? Or the frazzled housewife struggling to raise a family in a high-rise block of flats?

In truth, the essence of a true Dubliner is all of this and more. It's the Liffey as it flows by night, the hill of Howth on a clear blue day and the glorious flowers in the Botanic Gardens. It's the loud quick-witted bellow of the Moore Street trader, the lure of the Grafton Street busker, and the music, song and dance of Temple Bar.

But ultimately Dublin City is about people – the humourous, the poignant and the genial – who bring faces to places.

This book is not intended to be an in-depth analysis of Dublin life; rather it is a personal invitation to you, the reader, to engage in friendly conversation with some of our most distinguished citizens.

In this short collection I have attempted to capture just a little of that rare and extraordinary sense of belonging which endears Dublin to its people and goes some way to identifying the unique ingredients which make up its inhabitants.

Through dialogue with those who have impacted upon our nation in some way, we profile both those who have gone before us, and some of today's personalities in politics, social life, showbiz and music. Speaking openly and animatedly, those interviewed reflect on childhood memories, schooldays, families, hopes, dreams and ambitions. But most of all they speak of Dublin City, the place which generates deep emotion in the heart of all its children.

The Dublin experience

Many inhabitants and tourists see Dublin as one of the most attractive cities in Europe. Staking its claim as one of the world's most beautiful capitals, Dublin is blessed with majestic buildings, while the county boasts magnificent mountains and a wonderful shoreline along the Irish Sea.

Dublin houses a third of the country's entire population and is a vibrant, fast moving and highly cultural city, which is home to Ireland's most famous colleges and theatres.

The city's official date of establishment is 988 AD. The Norman Vikings were the first inhabitants, with the site later captured in the ninth century by the Danes, who were eventually expelled by the Anglo-Normans, led by Henry II, King of England, in 1171. In 1649, following the English Civil War, Dublin was taken over by Oliver Cromwell. It had a population of just 9,000 residents. Big changes lay ahead and towards the end of the seventeenth century, many Protestant refugees from the European continent arrived and the town showed the first signs of its global future. Although during this period it exuded vitality and wealth, Dublin suffered greatly through the abolishment of the 1800 Act of Union between Britain and Ireland. These hard times continued until the country eventually gained independence in 1922, the outcome of the 1916 Rising and the War of Independence. This was to pave the way for the gradual establishment of Dublin as the political, economic, and social centre of the country.

Bertie Ahern
Political Leader

Although thought of as a 'true blue Dub', Bertie Ahern was actually raised by parents who were natives of Cork city. Indeed, the Fianna Fáil leader and Taoiseach says that although he never acquired a Cork accent, his mother had it until the day she died. One of a family of five, Bertie Ahern was a pupil of St Patrick's, Drumcondra (a part of the teacher training college), and later attended nearby St Aidan's Christian Brothers School in Whitehall. Further education was received at the College of Commerce in Rathmines and at UCD, where he studied accountancy.

His father maintained his role as Farm Manager of All Hallows College all his life, allowing Bertie and his siblings the enviable privilege of a wide open playground unlike any other. 'There were horses, open spaces and a five-acre orchard,' he recalls. 'We were almost enticed by our folks to play there and I worked there as a student in the summer holidays as a farm labourer … it toughened me up!' he laughs. 'You don't appreciate it at the time, but looking back, to be living in Dublin and to have a rural lifestyle … it couldn't have been any better.'

Bertie speaks highly and affectionately of his parents, who raised him in

Drumcondra and who have both now passed away. 'My father and mother had very little money and they believed in education, so anything that they had went into education. They never went out, they never drank or smoked, they didn't socialise apart from going to friends' houses for a cup of tea. My father's only interest was the horses; he loved reading about them or listening to races on the radio. He went to the dogs – to Shelbourne Park and Harold's Cross – and bet a few shillings. He didn't put much money on because he hadn't got it. Our days out were at Croke Park – we had a huge interest in sport.' Bertie's love of sport, nurtured by his parents, is still evident today, despite his hectic schedule. 'We'd go to club matches featuring St Margaret's or St Vincent's, the college team at St Pat's. Or we'd walk to Fairview Park where there was an Irish night on a Sunday, or the Phoenix Park – that was the big day out!'

Throughout our conversation, Bertie Ahern speaks of the sense of intimacy that existed in Dublin when he was young. He laments that many of the open, green spaces are now gone, replaced by buildings. 'The parks are just about hanging in there,' he says. 'All the time there's more and more land being built on and it's sad. It's great in terms of generating activity and employment but the good old open spaces are all being slowly filled in and that is a great pity.'

Yet despite the faster pace of life today, Bertie believes that a strong community spirit can and will survive in Dublin. 'I suppose a great test is if you walk into a bar now in the middle of the city, the amount of people who would know you is not as great as it was (I suppose I'd be more known than most!). There are points of focus like the GAA club, places where you don't have to go with somebody, places where you can meet people. That sense of community is important. That's the strength that is the city and people don't always recognise it, but I do because I'm moving around so much. There is still a community based around the parish church, the parish schools and the clubs. I hope that community spirit remains. In some ways it is under threat but we should never lose it.'

Having been elected TD in 1977, Bertie served in several ministries before becoming Fianna Fáil leader. In 1994 he was elected Taoiseach. Now he finds himself attending engagements across the world, leading the country and striving for peace in Northern Ireland, but he still tries to find time to 'work around the parishes'. Indeed, from time to time he can be found enjoying a pint in his local in Drumcondra, cheering on the Dublin team at Croke Park, or opening a new school in the area – mixing with the people he was born amongst, the people who have supported him on his journey up the political ladder. 'It's what I like doing,' he states. 'I love people and I love the community. I very much relate to the community areas and the organisations. I tend to look at areas in that way – where is the community? Where is the parish? Where is the centre? Where are the clubs?'

Despite his hectic schedule at home and abroad, the Taoiseach still finds some time to pursue his various hobbies in a limited fashion. 'I run and jog a lot, though not as much as I used to … perhaps three or four days a week. I aim to get to bed by 12, but it's usually 1 and I'm up at 6.30 am … if I get five hours sleep I'm flying! And I love watching any kind of sport – rugby, soccer, Gaelic.'

His favourite place? 'Drumcondra,' he says immediately, that boyish grin spreading all over his animated face. 'I was born there, brought up there and I still live there. And All Hallows – I still go there for a walk or a run. I consider it to be a very special place, even though more and more of the land is being built on and it's getting smaller.'

Ahern's leadership has coincided with unprecedented prosperity for the country. 'I started preaching that there must be a better way, back when I was Lord Mayor and people were probably wondering what I was talking about!' he says. He explains that the social partnership approach has played a significant part in getting the economy right. 'There are three nice things about the good economy. Firstly, people who have never worked before are working, people have money in their pockets and it gives them a sense of dignity and achievement, it's good for their families and for their friends. The second thing is that we're able to build and develop things we never had before. The third thing is that we're now looking after people we never looked after before. We put a lot of money into schemes for the elderly, the disadvantaged, and the homeless. People say there's not enough but there are a whole lot of things going on – particularly when you're representing the inner city and the heart of the city, as I am, you see that very clearly.'

And what of other Dubliners? Who has been his biggest influence? 'Sean Lemass,' he says, confirming a well-documented personal admiration. 'He was the person I took a huge interest in when I was growing up, and I'm still reading about him today. Lemass has been my greatest influence and I still look at files here … and if anyone has read more about Lemass, I'd love to meet them!'

Molly Allgood

(Máire O'Neill)
—————————————Actress

Irish actress Molly Allgood was born in Dublin on 12 January 1887. On her father's death the youngster was sent to an orphanage and later apprenticed to a dressmaker. In 1905 she joined the Abbey Theatre where she met and befriended the man who would become besotted with her – John Millington Synge.

Taking the stage name Máire O'Neill she embarked on an exciting and impressive theatrical career, playing the role of Pegeen Mike in *The Playboy of the Western World*, to great acclaim in 1907.

After Synge's death, she took the lead role in his play *Deirdre of the Sorrows*. In 1911 she married the drama critic of the *Manchester Guardian* newspaper, George Herbert Mair, and they had two children, Pegeen and John.

With her personal life back on course, her career was also taking her on a new and adventurous journey, which included stints with the Liverpool Repertory Company, with Tree in Shakespeare in London, and with J. B. Fagan.

Mair died on 3 January 1926 and just six months later she married Abbey actor Arthur Sinclair, which whom she often appeared on stage, both in Dublin and in America.

In later life Allgood suffered great sorrow and hardship, through dependence on alcohol and a difficult marriage. The death of her son in an air accident added to her woes.

Molly Allgood passed away on 2 November 1952.

W. B. Yeats, in his Nobel Prize acceptance speech of 1923, referred to her as 'all simplicity'; and she can still be seen in the place she loved so well in a portrait by John Butler Yeats in the Abbey Theatre foyer.

Eamonn Andrews
Broadcaster

As he spent much of his successful career in the studios of the BBC and was a familiar adopted son to his UK audience, it may not be widely known that the man who made famous the presentation of the big red book in the popular show *This Is Your Life* was in fact a Dubliner.

Born in 1922, the young Eamonn Andrews was a student at the Holy Faith Convent in the Liberties and afterwards attended the Synge Street Christian Brothers School. He excelled at sports, particularly boxing, a sport he took up to protect himself from school bullies. He progressed to an advanced stage in the sport, winning the Irish junior middleweight title at the age of twenty-two.

His first job was as a clerk with the Hibernian Insurance Company in Dame Street, but he harboured a deep desire to work within the media. He finally got the chance to combine his two great loves when he began commentating on boxing matches on Radio Éireann. The articles he subsequently submitted to boxing magazines were made all the more absorbing by his obvious love of the sport.

By 1946 he was confident enough to pack in the day job and begin a career as a freelance broadcaster. Advancing from the sports desk to the world of entertainment, he became the popular host of *Question Time, Double or Nothing* and *Microphone Parade*, in which he interviewed celebrities of the day. His laid-back style and his ability to put his guests at ease made him the ideal choice as a talk show host.

Comfortably basking in the glory of his own success, Eamonn was quick to recognise his own potential – as were others. He relocated to London and became host of *Ignorance is Bliss* and *Sports Report*, remaining loyal to his own country by commuting on a regular basis and maintaining his place on Irish radio.

But it was for the BBC show *This is Your Life* that Eamonn Andrews became a household name and a much-loved face of television. In 1955 he became the show's first presenter. For many years he surprised musicians, actors, sports stars and those who had made a difference, recording their lives and times and never taking the spotlight away from his unsuspecting victims.

With a remarkable air of confidence and affable on-screen personality, Eamonn's talents were not confined to just one show and he presented the children's programme *Crackerjack* in addition to the radio talk show *Pied Piper*, revealing a unique capability for communicating with both young and old.

Despite his escalating career, his heart remained in Ireland and through his efforts the Eamonn Andrews Studios became a reality in Dublin. His immense personal popularity was evident when he received the top television personality awards in both 1956 and 1957 and, away from media circles, he was made a Knight of St Gregory in recognition of his ongoing charity work. He also demonstrated his business skills when the new Radio Éireann authority appointed him as its chairman. In 1970 he was rewarded the CBE.

Married to Gráinne Burke, Eamonn Andrews was so dedicated to his profession that he literally worked right up to the end. On 5 November 1987, he collapsed on the set of *What's My Line?* He died as he had lived, immersed in the love of his job, a quality that made this much-loved Dublin man a truly extraordinary broadcasting giant.

Dr Thomas Barnardo
Founder of Barnardos

Although it is widely believed that 'the old days' were safer times in which to raise children, child abuse and neglect have always been with us. While homelessness and poverty remain ongoing social dilemmas, the staunch work of many influential figures down through the years has been responsible for the establishment of some of today's most powerful and caring organisations.

Thomas John Barnardo was born at 4 Dame Street in 1845, the youngest of four boys. He was raised by kind and loving parents who instilled in him strong Christian values that were to be a major factor in the direction his life would later take. Sensitive, humble and kind-hearted, he expressed deep religious convictions and was 'born again' during a Protestant religious revival and became a preacher for many years.

Embarking on a medical career while developing a keen interest in social problems, he possessed an unrelenting spirit and a deep desire to care for and nurture the many children he observed living in desperation and destitution, both in Dublin and later in London. On witnessing horrific scenes of illness, terror and poverty, he abandoned previous plans to become a missionary, vowing instead to remain and do all in his power to aid the underprivileged.

Barnardo opened his first home for boys in Stepney Causeway, London, in 1870. Later he opened the Girls' Village Home in Barkingside. The cause of children's rights dominated Dr Barnardo's life, and as one home opened, another was being planned. Cafes and pubs were used as bases for volunteers to meet and congregate, and he remained undeterred by the phenomenal work involved and the sadness encountered along the way.

By the turn of the twentieth century Barnardo had rescued sixty thousand children from a life of oppression, going so far as to install safe houses and resettlement areas for children in Canada. Despite his good deeds, however, his actions were often looked upon with incredulity, leading to accusations of the misapplication of capital from various parties. Although officially cleared of these alleged offences, Dr Barnardo felt it wise to hand over his organisation to the care of trustees.

Unable to turn a child away from his door, Dr Thomas Barnardo displayed a tremendous charitable disposition, defiantly working for 'his' children until he died of heart failure in 1905.

His legacy proudly lives on in the many Barnardos homes that today care for the generations of lost souls in his name. For this gift he will never be forgotten – Dublin adopts his name with pride, with 4 Dame Street and 108 Grafton Street paying tribute to the work of a selfless and irreplaceable messenger.

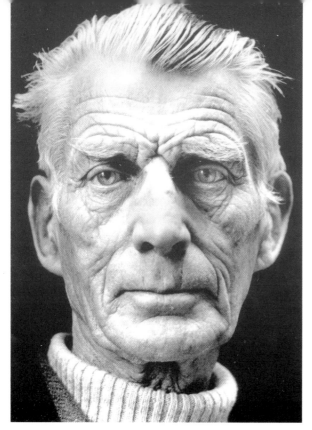

Samuel Beckett
————————Playwright

Born on Good Friday, 13 April 1906, in Brighton Road, Foxrock, Samuel Beckett remains one of the powerful literary voices of the twentieth century.

He was raised in a middle-class Protestant home, the son of a quantity surveyor and a nurse. He attended the same school as fellow scribe Oscar Wilde prior to entering Trinity College. A somewhat disturbed young man, Beckett was tormented by feelings of loneliness and was often bedridden and withdrawn through deep depression. He seemed to wallow in his own solitude and was reluctant to invite others into his life – he revealed that after rejecting advances from James Joyce's daughter, Lucia, he felt 'dead and had no feelings that were human'.

In 1928, Beckett moved to Paris, a romantic city he would come to regard with some affection. It was in this environment that he first encountered James Joyce, who welcomed him into an exclusive literary social circle. This inclusion went some way to fulfilling his immense hunger for success, and at just twenty-three he penned an essay in defence of Joyce's *Ulysses* against the public's lazy demand for easy comprehensibility. At twenty-four he claimed his first literary prize – of £10 for his poem entitled 'Whoroscope' (on philosopher Descartes' meditation on the subject of time and the transience of life).

In time, however, Beckett grew disillusioned with life in Paris and set out to see the world, embarking on a nomadic journey across Europe, taking in Ireland, France, England and Germany and encountering many different characters, who were to be the inspiration for much of his future writing. He did odd jobs and wrote poems and short stories to survive.

Despite the distance between them, Beckett and Joyce maintained their close bond and enjoyed an easy and relaxed friendship for many years. Beckett returned to Paris in 1937. During World War II he combined his great love for writing with another passion – he fought for the resistance until 1942, when some members of his group were arrested and he had to flee with his French-born wife Suzanne Dumesnil to the unoccupied zone. For his part in the resistance, he was to become the worthy recipient of the exclusive Croix de Guerre award.

Following the liberation of Paris from the Germans in 1945, Beckett returned there and, as soon as time permitted, resumed his writing. He produced *Eleutheria, Malone Dies, Molloy, The Unnamable* and *Mercier et Camier*, closely followed by a number of short and less publicised works for both radio and television. Theatrical offerings included *Endgame*, which premiered in French at the Royal Court Theatre in London, *Happy Days, Come and Go* and the unique *Breath*, which only lasted an incredible thirty seconds.

The late 1940s saw the production of Beckett's best work. All of his writings were originally in French – apparently because he wanted the discipline and economy of expression that an acquired language would force upon him. Most of his characters were introverted and misunderstood people, perhaps as a result of his own personal experiences.

In 1953 he struck gold with his masterpiece *Waiting for Godot*. This sensational play incorporated a wonderful mix of serious drama, comedy and tragedy. It premiered at the Théâtre de Babylone and became an instant success, running for four hundred performances and attracting critical acclaim from dramatists Tennessee Williams, Thornton Wilder and William Saroyan, who was heard to say: 'It will make it easier for me and everyone else to write freely in the theatre.'

To date the works of Samuel Beckett have been translated into over twenty languages, but, despite the scale of his success, he was never comfortable with fame and was even heard to say he felt more comfortable with failure! He shied away from social occasions, including the official ceremony at which he was awarded the Nobel Prize for Literature in 1969.

Although he continued to write up to the time of his death in 1989 (just five months after the death of his beloved Suzanne), the task grew more and more difficult, and in the end he said each word seemed to him 'an unnecessary stain on silence and nothingness'.

Brendan Behan
Writer

Brendan Behan had many demons. He spent time in prison, fell victim to alcoholism and encountered many bouts of profound unhappiness. Sadly, it seems fair to presume that his brilliance as a creative writer brought more pleasure to others than to himself.

Brendan Behan was born in 1923 into a republican working-class family living in Russell Street, and at a later stage moving to Kimmage. At Behan's birth, his father was in a British compound on charges arising from the Irish fight for independence. At the tender age of eight, Behan voiced his political inclinations by joining the IRA youth wing, Fianna Éireann. His mother instilled in him her love of traditional Irish ballads, and his father, who was a keen reader, sowed the first seeds of his son's interest in the arts and literature.

Boasting a fierce sense of patriotic determination and outspokenness, which never failed to attract attention – and not all of it good – Behan left school at fourteen years of age, evolving into a troubled young man who forged a somewhat hostile relationship with the authorities. He was actively involved with the IRA and was arrested several times in his youth, resulting in an anger and bitterness that was to fester within him for some time, eventually erupting in a series of turbulent incidents. In 1939 he was arrested on a sabotage mission in England and sentenced to three years in Borstal reform school for smuggling explosives from Ireland to Liverpool in an IRA attempt to blow up a battleship in Liverpool harbour. After release he returned to Ireland, but in 1942 he was sentenced to fourteen years for the attempted murder of two detectives outside Glasnevin cemetery. He served at Mountjoy Prison and at the Curragh Military Camp. In 1946 he was released under a general amnesty. He was in prison again in Manchester in 1947, serving a short term for allegedly helping an IRA prisoner to escape. During his years in prison, Behan began to write, mainly short stories in an inventive stylisation of the Dublin vernacular. He later analysed his time in prison and the people he encountered with more than a hint of humour: 'The English are wonderful – first they put me in jail and then they made me rich!'

1952 saw him in France, where he settled in Paris for some time, writing pornography for French magazines, as well as doing bar work and house painting to help make ends meet. By the time he returned to his native land, he had made a name as an accomplished writer and balladeer, and he produced his first play, *The Quare Fella*, in 1954. This was closely followed by *The Hostage*. Both were critically acclaimed and were staged in Britain, Paris, Berlin and America.

Borstal Boy, his most famous work, was published in 1958. It is the moving account of his experiences as a sixteen-year-old in the Liverpool jail and his time in Borstal. The young narrator moves from rebellious bravado to a greater understanding of himself and the world.

With the success of his writing, Behan felt the pressures of life as a figure of attention, and he turned to alcohol, which somehow helped to ease the burdens of success and fame. Drink may have been his best friend but it ultimately played the part of his worst enemy too. Behan frequently let himself down in public when drunk.

His relationship with the bottle tainted a once unblemished image and inflicted irreparable damage on his body, inevitably contributing to his eventual decline. Despite falling into ill health, Behan's mind remained brilliant and alert until the end, and when he could no longer write physically, he chose to record his thoughts and words on tape, which today remains a precious and wonderful legacy of his genius.

Willie Bermingham
Social activist

Willie Bermingham was a fireman who, like many others, attended the scenes of accidents and rescued victims from blazing houses. But for this extraordinary man, born in Bluebell, Inchicore in 1943, it was nigh on impossible to escape the haunting images witnessed and the graphic memories of charred bodies killed in horrific circumstances, all too often in the poorest areas of the city.

Fuelled by a deep inner strength and a personal sense of anger and injustice, Bermingham founded ALONE ('A Little Offering Never Ends') in 1977. Armed with a fierce determination and a willingness to speak for those who didn't have a voice, this compassionate man campaigned tirelessly to provide essential clothing, shelter, food and the basic necessities required by the less fortunate.

His perseverance paid off and the government could no longer ignore the pleas and unbreakable spirit of one individual who represented so many others. A task force was established with the prime intention of alleviating the pain of the downtrodden. In 1986 ALONE campaigners saw the fruits of their labour with the completion of a spacious and much needed eleven-house complex in Artane, operating a regular distribution of resources to those facing neglect and ruin. Just a week before Willie's death, he turned the sod on a twenty-two unit housing scheme in Kilmainham.

Although he never sought it, the work and dedication of this angel of mercy attracted great recognition and the reluctant Dubliner was the worthy recipient of a number of illustrious awards, including the International Fireman of the Year, a People of the Year Award in 1979 and an Honorary LL.D. from Trinity College in 1988.

At just forty-eight years of age, Willie Bermingham passed away, but he left an inspirational legacy of love and tolerance. His selfless devotion to the abandoned lives on in the work of ALONE.

Maeve Binchy
—————————————Novelist

One of the most popular novelists to emerge from Ireland, Maeve Binchy was born and raised in Dalkey, Co Dublin.

Her climb up the ladder to success began shortly after she received her BA from University College, Dublin, and embarked on a teaching career. However, it was when her father sold one of her moving and graphic letters from a trip abroad to *The Irish Times* for a greater sum than her weekly earnings, that the young Maeve knew she had hit upon something special. More letters followed and she emerged as a popular columnist with readers of all ages.

While writing for *The Irish Times*, Maeve began work on her first novel, *Light a Penny Candle*, which was published in 1983. It was an instant success. More was to follow, with *Evening Class*, *The Glass Lake*, *The Copper Beech*, *Firefly Summer*, *The Lilac Bus*, *Echoes*, *Silver Wedding*, and *Tara Road*, while the bestselling *Circle of Friends* was recreated on the big screen with Minnie Driver and Chris O'Donnell in the starring roles.

Proof of Maeve Binchy's great appeal came when she received a phone call at her home from a woman with a heavy American accent claiming to be Oprah Winfrey. 'I thought it was one of my friends having a go,' she says humorously. 'I said "Oh yeah, really, who is this?" And she said, "It is Oprah," in a very heavy voice and I knew it was, so I straightened my back and said, "Well, how are you?" And we chatted away.'

Why was the most famous woman in America calling a Dublin number? Maeve Binchy's latest novel, *Tara Road*, which follows the fortunes and friendship of two very different Irish women over the course of their lifetime, had apparently been chosen for inclusion in Miss Winfrey's prestigious book club. Maeve's subsequent appearance on the Oprah Winfrey show in Chicago was an unforgettable experience.

While Binchy's writing may be criticised from time to time as being 'easy', in truth, it is far from 'easy'. She has few peers in her field. She writes with terrific feel for people, families, relationships and situations. Maeve refers to her brief conversation with a lady she encountered one day on the street, who stated dismissively: 'Sure, I could write that!' 'Ah yes, but I did write it!' was the simple retort.

Despite the incredible success of her career, Maeve is content to live a relatively simple life in the place she grew up in, Dalkey, with her husband Gordon Snell.

Christy Brown
Writer

Born with uncooperative limbs and an impotent body as a result of cerebral palsy, Christy Brown was a remarkable man. He steadfastly refused to allow severe physical disabilities to adversely affect or impair his extraordinary intellect and his burning desire to write.

Born into a large family in Stannaway Road, Crumlin, in 1932, Christy's astonishing potential was recognised and nurtured by his mother, who gave birth to twenty-two children, thirteen of whom survived. Defiantly dismissing the devastating medical diagnosis that predicted no real future for her son, Mrs Brown refused to have him placed in an institution and vowed to care for her child at home. This was to herald a new beginning for the young Christy, who one day determinedly seized a piece of chalk between the toes of his left foot and drew the outline of a letter. Spurred on by his mother's unfailing belief, he persevered until he could write.

His autobiography, *My Left Foot*, was published in 1954, when he was just twenty-two years old. It was expanded into the novel *Down All the Days* in 1976 and became an international bestseller, translated into fourteen languages. The novel provides a poignant insight into an unconventional and at times quite lonely childhood. He gave real meaning to an often undignified and misunderstood life of dependence, at times tortured by his own limitations. 'That one letter,' he stated later, 'was my road to a new world – my key to mental freedom.'

There followed other novels, including *A Shadow on Summer* (1976). He also published a number of poetry collections, including *Of Snails and Skylarks* and *Background Music*.

In 1989 Jim Sheridan made a film of *My Left Foot,* starring Daniel Day Lewis and Brenda Fricker.

For all his international recognition, Christy Brown was an ordinary man who fought for equality. This he discovered through the intimacy of his relationship with nurse Mary Carr, who became his wife in 1972. They settled in Ballyheigue, Co Kerry and also in Parbrook, Somerset, where he died in 1981.

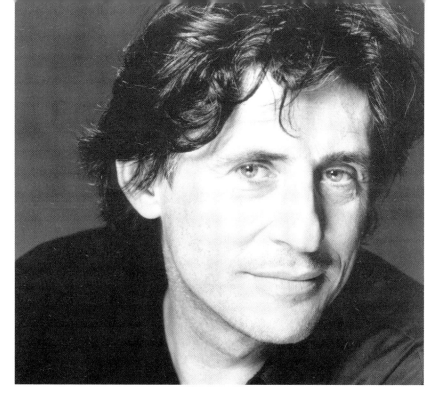

Gabriel Byrne

Actor

Heart-throb, superstar and actor – just some of the labels attached to a man who has travelled far and wide and who today enjoys the bright lights of Hollywood. Gabriel Byrne has come a long way from Walkinstown in what has been an extraordinary and absorbing journey. Today he enjoys fame and fortune and is instantly recognisable as one of the all-time Irish acting greats.

The eldest in a family of six, Gabriel was born in 1950. His father worked in the Guinness brewery and his mother Eileen was a nurse. Talented and enterprising as a child, he excelled at both music and drama, expressing a strong and unrelenting desire to perform and impress. He attended the Drimnagh Castle Christian Brothers School and St Richard's College in England, before winning a scholarship to UCD, which brought him back home.

At UCD this promising scholar embarked upon a lengthy course of study, incorporating subjects as diverse as languages and archaeology, while in his spare time writing and composing fiction and prose for radio and developing an active involvement in publishing.

It was during this period that Byrne made his theatrical debut, starring in *Coriolanus* in 1976 with the Dublin Shakespeare Society. He also played some minor roles in the city's Focus Theatre. He got his first big chance to prove his potential with a role in *The Liberty Suit* by Mannix Flynn, with further appearances following in the Abbey. However, it was for his part in RTÉ's *The Riordans* and later *Bracken* that he made his name, a broody presence who was quickly tipped to go further.

He went on to excel dramatically in many BBC productions of the 1980s and progressed to big-screen success with *The Rocking Horse* and *Defence of the Realm*. Byrne revealed a unique ability to depict a succession of conflicting emotions in *Miller's Crossing* and the endearing *Into the West*, filmed on location in Ireland. When one adds his performances in *The Man in the Iron Mask*, *The Usual Suspects*, *Little Women* and *End of Days*, his versatility cannot be questioned. Whether playing the rural farmer or the undercover investigative journalist, the arrogant mobster or Satan himself, Gabriel Byrne has been the recipient of much critical acclaim.

Byrne, despite his phenomenal showbiz success, remains a family man at heart. Though he separated amicably from his wife, Ellen Barkin, he remains very much a committed father and is currently based full-time in America, although he maintains close contacts with his native country.

Byrne has also worked on the other side of the cameras, as co-producer in the Oscar-winning production *In the Name of the Father*. He also published *Pictures in My Head* in 1996, his poignant rendition of a deeply emotional letter to his daughter, both momentous and heartrending.

But it is for his unparalleled screen presence that he will always be known – a gifted and versatile actor.

Gay Byrne

Broadcaster

Born in 1934 in Donore Avenue, Rialto, Gay Byrne was one of a family of five and received his early education in Synge Street Christian Brothers School. Raised in a family that consisted almost entirely of Guinness Brewery employees, the young Gay seemed predestined for a similar vocation, yet it wasn't to be, as he explains with just a little regret. 'My father worked in Guinness, my brother, my uncles, cousin, sister all did too, but I failed the entrance exam!'

This initial setback steered the industrious Gabriel into the insurance business (starting as a salesman with the Royal Irish Company in Dame Street), before his great love for the film and theatrical world took over. He switched jobs and took up a new role as trainee manager at the Odeon Cinema on O'Connell Street. He remained in this position for several years but, although he enjoyed it and the wages were good, he became disheartened by the long hours and eventually opted to return to insurance.

However, happily for future generations of Irish people, fate had other plans in store. The personable and ambitious Gay Byrne would not be confined to a life of selling insurance policies. He got a job with RTÉ, presenting short sponsored programmes and the news. He later took something of a gamble and moved to the UK, where he found work with Granada Television. Although he confesses 'I knew nothing about television,' he went on to charm the powers that be with his determination and a laid-back style that would prove to find favour with management and the viewing public. Indeed, so impressed were Granada that they paid his airfare home to Dublin every weekend! 'It was a fantastic training ground,' he enthuses. A further three years experience was then gained with the BBC in London before Gay returned to the Emerald Isle where what would prove to be a remarkable and long-standing alliance with RTÉ began in 1958.

Soon he had his own modern weekly talk programme – *The Late Late Show*. This groundbreaking show initiated discussion, fuelled controversy and gave a voice to the anonymous as well as the celebrity. Incredibly, the show would continue with Byrne as host for over three decades. He also produced the show for a number of years. An astonishingly popular and influential programme, the 'Late Late' played its part in liberalising a changing country. In addition to highlighting countless social issues, the show featured interviews with world-famous celebrities and of course acted as a forum for many up-and-coming entertainers. Developing an incredible following in its heyday, the show became an Irish institution, as did its host.

Despite offers from British television stations and a flirtation with the US chat show circuit at the peak of his fame, this patriotic Dubliner could not be tempted to leave Ireland. Instead he remained at home, combining his television career with an equally brilliant and lengthy tenure as radio broadcaster.

Eventually in the late 1990s, with Gay Byrne now in his early sixties, the era came to an end. Gay vacated the Late Late chair.

A Dubliner through and through, it's hardly surprising therefore that his home is in a favourite part of this city. 'I adore Howth,' he says, 'and I couldn't imagine living anywhere else. It's a fantastic place, unique, absolutely wonderful and I walk my dogs there most days.' And perhaps it's that sense of belonging that endears this particular area to him. Gay has witnessed many changes in the city of course. 'It has grown so enormously,' he said. 'I used to drive into RTÉ along a completely deserted road. Now it seems it's rush hour all the time.'

If the image of Gay Byrne sauntering briskly along the hill of Howth with his two dogs in tow is a little unrealistic for you, how about the sight of a leather-clad

Gaybo speeding down the hill on a dream motorcycle? On his final *Late Late Show*, Gay famously received the gift of a Harley Davidson bike from U2. It has been tested – and often. 'People thought it would just gather dust in a shed,' he laughs. 'But I got my licence and I've done 12,000 miles on it. The freedom is terrific; I'm out on it all the time. I'm in a helmet, no-one knows who I am and I look like your average courier!'

We switch our conversation to heroes and idols, and without hesitation Gay Byrne delivers his choice of his favourite. 'Eamonn Andrews was my hero. He was a great friend of my mother's and used to visit our house. He was great at the racing commentary and became a great star – I always wanted to be like him.'

Alas one ambition remains as yet unfulfilled. Of all the people he has interviewed, one enigmatic and beautiful lady never quite got the Gaybo treatment. 'Meryl Streep,' he sighs. 'She almost came, but the fog descended and she never made it. It wasn't to be,' he says, 'but she did send me a nice note afterwards and I sent her one back. So evidently the spark is still there!'

Although Gay Byrne's retirement from *The Late Late Show* and from his radio show was sad for his legions of fans, for him it is a personal bonus as he finally salvaged time for himself, reading, cycling or spending time with his wife Kathleen. 'For many years myself and Kathleen could never go away together because from the first of September to the end of June I was working, but since then I've been to London, to America, to Egypt, to New York and to Donegal. I have no regrets.' He's obviously enjoying life immensely. And if the correspondence and attention he receives is anything to go by, he is gone, but not forgotten! 'The post is ferocious,' he exclaims, in reference to the phenomenal number of people who request his input into various projects. Clearly his high level of popularity has not diminished in any sense. Now the multi-award-winning presenter is juggling 'retirement' with his hosting of *Who Wants to be a Millionaire?*, ensuring he will be introduced to younger generations – adding further chapters to his great success story.

Gay's former colleague and current presenter of *Liveline*, Joe Duffy, states: 'There is only one certainty about Gay Byrne and that is he is the greatest broadcaster ever in Ireland. As Irish broadcasting develops, there can never be a more influential figure because even with today's broadcasting, with satellite TV, etc., nobody can ever have the impact that Gay Byrne had when he started in RTÉ. It's as simple as that.'

Edward Carson
Lawyer and politician

Unionist leader and lawyer Edward Carson, the man largely responsible for the establishment of Northern Ireland, was, ironically, born and bred in the South. The second son of a Dublin architect, Carson was raised in Harcourt Street and educated at Portarlington School and later attended Trinity College.

After graduating with a degree in law, Carson set up his practice at Herbert Place, later expanding to Merrion Square in response to the demands of a burgeoning clientele. However, the life of a lawyer was not challenging enough to satisfy the ambitious mind and political inclinations of this formidable man.

Carson became solicitor-general for Ireland in 1892 and was elected as a Liberal Unionist for Dublin University. He later moved to London where he was an active legal representative. One of his most memorable cases was representing the Marquess of Queensberry in his allegations against Oscar Wilde. Carson and Wilde had been friends for a brief time while at Trinity College, Dublin, and Wilde commented sarcastically, 'No doubt he will perform his task with all the bitterness of an old friend.' And indeed he did – with the result that his own career reached new heights and Oscar Wilde was led away to the cells, convicted on charges of homosexual tendencies and acts of indecency.

With his political ambitions taking root, Carson was later elected leader of the Irish Unionist Parliamentary Party and founded the Ulster Volunteers, which saw him bear responsibility for the smuggling of arms and ammunition into Larne.

He held strong and controversial views, believing that ultimately no plans for devolution could possibly go ahead without any one part of the country – 'If Ulster secedes, Home Rule is dead,' he warned.

This well-respected, intelligent and resourceful political leader developed a strong following and remained a resolute and decisive man who was a fighting force for any opposition. The passing of the Home Rule Bill in 1914 meant that just twenty-six counties gained independence, a fact Carson took as a personal failure. Despite this turn of events, Carson remained committed and active in his cause and, although he resigned his leadership of the UUP in 1921, he sustained a position of authority in the House of Commons for over thirty years before entering the Upper House as Lord Carson of Duncairn.

Roger Casement
Patriot

Sir Roger David Casement was born in Dublin in 1864. His was a hard childhood. His father died when he was a babe in arms and his mother when he was nine, at which point he and his siblings were sent to live with their uncle John Casement in Antrim. There the young boy received his education in the Diocesan School in Ballymena.

As soon as he came of age, Roger got his first job in the office of the Elder Dempster Shipping Line and sailed to Africa, later joining the British colonial service. He spent the next two decades in Africa and became a campaigning voice against the appalling living conditions he witnessed there. His efforts in exposing the exploitation of native workers by European employers in Africa and South America earned him a knighthood in 1911 and, although he eagerly accepted the award, he was privately heard to comment that 'There are many in Ireland will think of me as a traitor and when I think of that country and of them, I feel I am.'

It wasn't until 1913 that Casement found his way back home again and became embroiled in the political life of his country, revealing a deep commitment to the pursuit of Irish independence. He helped to set up the Irish Volunteers in a gesture of opposition to Carson's Ulster Volunteers and spent the next couple of years seeking support from Germany. However, their offer was considered insufficient by Casement, and he returned to Ireland to postpone the Easter Rebellion.

After his landing from a German submarine in Tralee Bay on Good Friday, 21 April 1916, he was immediately arrested and tried for treason. He was subsequently condemned to death, despite support and impassioned pleas for leniency from influential figures of the time, including Conan Doyle, G. K. Chesterson, W. B. Yeats and George Bernard Shaw. In a determined effort to further blacken his name, some British agents exposed extracts from his diaries detailing homosexual activity, and their unearthing put an end to any hopes of reprieve. Although the diaries were probably genuine, the nature of their use helped to inspire controversy about the possibility of forgery.

Sir Roger Casement was hanged for treason on 3 August 1916. Almost fifty years later, in 1965, his courage and fighting spirit were finally acknowledged and his body was returned to its rightful place and reinterred in Glasnevin cemetery.

Anthony Clare
Psychiatrist

'I'm terribly cynical! I never believe a word economists say because I don't think they know what they're talking about. I always say they're a bit like psychiatrists!' says Dublin city's most famous psychiatrist, Professor Anthony Clare, seated in his spacious consulting room in St Patrick's Hospital, James's Street, where he is Head of Psychiatry.

Today's Dublin is a far cry from the Dublin of Anthony Clare's youth. Brought up in Ranelagh, the son of a state solicitor, he attended Gonzaga College. He developed a keen interest in medicine in his late teens and studied it at University College, Dublin.

So what did he think of Dublin in 'the rare oul times'? 'People had less,' he states plainly. 'At the moment the past is getting a bad deal and we're all concentrating on how bleak it was and how glum and how boring Dublin was. But there were good things as well – friendship was strong, home and family were strong and they were important. Indeed we're worrying about how we can protect them in this "New

Ireland". My parents lived in a much simpler city and they lived much simpler lives, but they knew that buying a house wouldn't cripple them. Now here we are, some forty or fifty years later, much wealthier – yet my own sons and daughters find it hard to buy the most fundamental basic requirements.'

Clare sees many positive aspects to the cultural developments in Dublin. 'The biggest single change is the sheer proliferation of things to do. There's a tremendous vitality and we are slowly developing an alternative to the drinking culture.'

He agrees that the old Dublin may have been gravely lacking in financial security and the luxuries of life, but having analysed the situation, he remains adamant in his desire for the rebirth of a stable, family-oriented society. He refers to the fact that his mother knew everyone else who lived on their street. 'Dublin was always made up of a collection of communities, the northside and southside were never joined, but places like Phibsboro, Killester, Clontarf, Howth, Drumcondra, Finglas, Cabra, they were all so different, and the question therefore is "Are there still communities within Dublin?" I don't know,' he concludes after a brief hesitation. 'I wonder how many people know each other now in Ranelagh or Palmerston Park or Ballsbridge or Ringsend? "Ranelagh village?" God help us all!' he says dramatically.

Families are high on the list of priorities for an individual who expertly manages to juggle a career as a working psychiatrist, broadcaster, author, devoted husband to Jane and father of seven children. 'Families and extended families did spend much more time together – it did have its downside: some families were absolutely ghastly and pathological and people couldn't wait to get away from them. But in general, there was a strong emphasis on family, on people and on social interaction, and when you've been abroad in a country like Britain for twenty years, you see the difference.'

Staying with the theme of social interaction, he says, 'The Irish people will sacrifice anything for a party and good luck to them! I think that's not a bad thing in proportion, whereas in Britain social interaction comes low on the list, after work, your possessions or your pension. I'm exaggerating of course, but I do hope we don't become like that.'

Currently resident in Lucan, Clare exudes a deep affection for Dublin city, though he singles out areas that are in major need of improvement. 'O'Connell Street is still a mess, both in terms of the way it's laid out and in terms of the shops on it. The traffic is an absolute disaster, the taxi arrangements in the city are a joke, the litter is appalling, the whole way of looking at the city leaves a lot to be desired.'

Dublin's crime rate has risen considerably in recent years, an issue Dr Clare confronts from the viewpoint of someone who has himself been a victim. Despite this highly publicised and traumatic attack, which occurred in his own home, he retains the view that hysteria can reign where common sense ought to prevail. 'I think you can get these things out of proportion and you can start to breed an atmosphere of panic. People say, "I'd never go to the cinema in O'Connell Street," and that sort of nonsense, but Dublin is no different from the rest of the world and the worst thing you can do is to withdraw from the centre of the city. That's what happened in America. They turned the city centres into highway exchanges and the result was that they became ghastly places.'

Very much in tune with and somewhat emotionally attached to the places he encountered as a child, Anthony Clare still enjoys brief periods of recreation in visits to Donabate beach and Sandymount strand. Here he recaptures precious childhood memories, varying slightly from those of his immediate family. 'I was away a lot and so my children were much more aware of France and Italy and were very lucky. It was a different experience. Of course today's kids aren't going to Donabate beach, they're going to Malibu and Ibiza!' he adds. 'But I love the sea and would like to live closer to there one day. I love the mountains and the north coast; the Liffey Valley in Lucan is beautiful. I love flying into Dublin on a summer's day and seeing the layout of the city.'

Confessing to being spoilt for choice when selecting his own heroes, he does, however, attribute great credit to James Joyce, while harbouring a deep fondness and sense of admiration for Dubliners in general. 'I used to have a much stronger Dublin accent and it got lost down through the years,' he claims. 'I love the Dublin humour — O'Casey and Joyce. The average Dubliners from Gardiner Street and the Coombe are wary, captivating and humorous. They don't put their faith in money or buildings. That's where Dublin is different. It's a fine city but not a grand city like Paris. Dubliners don't take themselves too seriously and they won't get corrupted by all this gold and the Celtic Tiger. I like the Dubliner,' he concludes, grinning mischievously.

Ronan Collins
Broadcaster

For RTÉ broadcaster Ronan Collins, Dublin city invariably conjures up poignant memories of his close relationship with his father, who passed away just a year before this interview, a traumatic period in his life which today evokes a noticeably emotional response. 'My father worked in the army barracks,' he says softly. 'He died late last year and I miss him terribly. You prepare yourself for bereavement but it's still really hard. We got so close in later years.' He recalls with just a hint of a smile how one of his nephews reacted to the sorrowful news. 'But who's going to sit in *his* chair?' the boy queried dramatically, in reference to his grandfather's 'special place' in the house, a chair which defined his powerful presence. Today Ronan and other visiting members of the family who call to see his mother regularly, preserve the priceless memory of his father by constantly occupying that chair. 'We talk about him all the time,' he says. 'He's always there.'

Born in Shandon Park, Phibsboro, Ronan was one of a family of six children, and as a teenager he attended St Vincent's School, Glasnevin. 'I wasn't academically inclined,' he says on reflection. 'I had no concept of the bigger picture and couldn't wait to get out of school.' He was more interested in becoming a DJ. The young Collins developed a natural ability to succeed in the music industry and set about making a name for himself. 'I got a summer job in town, in a jewellers, but my first "proper job" didn't come along for a long time because I was playing music and working as a disc jockey. I got a job as a computer programmer for a company that made marmalade!' His deep love for the music scene is evident from the many years spent playing the drums in show bands and is equalled only by a similar affection for theatre and film, an interest still apparent in weekly outings to the cinema with his wife and young children.

Although a now well-recognised face with regular weekly slots on RTÉ television, in addition to a popular daily radio broadcast, Ronan is a man who somehow manages to preserve his privacy. He tries to achieve the difficult balance between a personal and professional life. 'My professional life revolves around radio and television and I believe that if you choose to do that, you put yourself up for criticism and you've got to accept it. But by and large no one bothers me. If I'm out for a meal with my wife and someone asks for the Lotto numbers, it doesn't bother me. I'm not a controversial person. People don't give me a hard time and I don't want to be a millionaire or be famous.'

When it comes to Dublin, Ronan Collins expresses little or no sentiment about the gradual 'disappearance' of Dublin. Instead he philosophically accepts it as an inevitable sign of progress. One point of irritation he does have in common with many of his fellow city-dwellers, however, is the traffic problem in the city – a constant source of deep frustration for commuters. 'There just aren't enough car parks on the fringe of the city,' he says. 'Nobody can park anywhere.' Speaking of the woes of travelling and securing parking spaces, this Dubliner has taken the dramatic move of actually lengthening his daily journey to and from work by moving from the city to County Meath. This saw him bid farewell to the heart of Dublin's northside for the first time, and enter an environment generally considered 'to offer a better way of life'. Acknowledging Dublin's biggest and most potentially destructive problem as being the scourge of drug addiction, he feels that in times gone by, 'there were other distractions instead' that were obviously not as damaging.

In terms of influences on his career, one showbiz legend in particular remains a favourite. 'There have been lots of Dublin people, but I've always admired Dickie Rock, from the days when I was a drummer in a band in Cabra. He's a Dublin icon. I also admire Peter O'Neill of the *Sunday World* and Bono, who brought new life to rock and roll.'

William T. Cosgrave
Statesman

Wiilliam Thomas Cosgrave was born in 1880 at 174 James's Street and was first introduced to politics by his father – a publican and politician, who watched with pride as his son went on to achieve great success. Cosgrave was one of the delegates to the first convention of Arthur Griffith's Sinn Féin in the Rotunda, Dublin, in 1905. With the emergence of the party in Dublin, he was elected councillor to Dublin Corporation in 1909. He joined the Irish Volunteers in 1913 and fought in the 1916 Easter Rising, narrowly escaping death when his sentence was commuted to imprisonment. He was released in the general amnesty of 1917.

He won the Carlow-Kilkenny seat for Sinn Féin in 1917 and sat in the first Dáil. He was appointed Minister for Local Government from 1919 to 1922. As a staunch supporter of the Treaty, he succeeded Michael Collins as Chairman of the Provisional Government and Minister for Finance in July 1922, and in August 1922 he succeeded Arthur Griffith as president of the Dáil. The high esteem in which he was held resulted in his appointment as first President of the Executive Council of the Free State. It was a role he embraced with an unbreakable spirit. He stood undeterred by growing opposition from pro-British quarters and was determined to right the wrongs imposed on his country. He played a crucial part in the creation of hope for a new beginning and a welcome state of democracy for the Irish people.

During his period as President of the Executive Council, Cosgrave initiated real and positive change, restoring the foundation of an unarmed civic police force – An Garda Síochána – in addition to a national army loyal to the State. One of his most notable and worthwhile achievements was in persuading the majority of those opposed to the Treaty to reject militarism in favour of parliamentary democracy. Cosgrave was also instrumental in the peaceful transfer of power to Fianna Fáil in 1932, and his stint as leader of Fine Gael from 1934 lasted a full decade.

On his retirement, William T. Cosgrave devoted more time to his hobby of stud farming. He died in 1965 and was given a state funeral to Goldenbridge cemetery in Inchicore.

Shay Cullen
Missionary

For over thirty years one Irish man has challenged and confronted the evils of a lucrative child sex industry in the Philippines. It's a long way from his native Dublin home and this courageous and difficult crusade has seen Fr Shay Cullen face accusations of libel, slander and even rape that could have led to the death penalty had it not been decisively proven to be false. 'But,' says Fr Shay Cullen, matter of factly, 'this is an occupational hazard. It's part of the job.'

Born in Dublin on 27 March 1943, the youngest in a family of seven, Shay Cullen was a pupil of the Harold Schools (Elementary) Glasthule, the Christian Brothers, Monkstown Park and the Presentation College, Sandycove. He entered St Columban's Seminary, Dalgan Park, Navan, Co Meath in 1963 and was ordained to the priesthood six years later, as a member of the Missionary Society of St Columban.

Fr Shay's very first assignment was to change his life – and that of many others – forever. On arrival in St Joseph's Church, Olongapo City, in 1969, he was immediately confronted with the colossal social and human problems caused by the sex industry, which thrived beside a US Navy base. Sexual abuse of children was commonplace and the naval base was eventually closed down as a direct result of his campaigning. His vision to convert the huge facilities into an industrial park succeeded and brought about the collapse of the sex industry and the provision of dignified jobs for thousands of Filipinos.

Following brief periods back in Ireland and with Mother Teresa in Calcutta, Fr Cullen returned to the Philippines in 1972 where he took up further language studies and trained in the operation and management of a Drug Rehabilitation Centre. He then returned to Olongapo City, north west of Manila and founded PREDA (People's Recovery, Empowerment and Development Assistance Foundation, Inc.) in 1974, with the co-operation of Merly Ramirez Hermoso and Alex Corpus Hermoso.

Through this organisation, committed to helping abused children and working for human rights and development, Cullen comes face to face with the horrors and evils of child sexual abuse on a daily basis. Living with a professional team of dedicated Filipino colleagues, he has established a reputation which has made his name a familiar one to faith groups, Non-Governmental Organisations (NGOs) and solidarity movements and authorities worldwide in the battle against paedophilia.

'I do not assume a father role in the sense that I see the children as "my own",' he says. 'That doesn't mean that I don't feel concern, of course I do; but the appropriate response is not to "own" them (the children) in any way, but to restore them to health and reintegrate them with their families and the love of their own home.'

In attempting to explain what motivates him to help the oppressed, he goes back to his own childhood and what drew him to accept the call. 'It was the challenge of a different and adventurous life in the great unknown that attracted me at first, but the example of Jesus Christ was the overwhelming influence,' he says. 'I realised how privileged I was, just to be basically secure and to have a education. When I read about the oppression and injustice, I felt I wanted to do something meaningful and worthwhile with my life and bring some small change to the lives of these people. It was no one thing, no "Road to Damascus" experience, but a combination of these important realities. I thought it a good thing to do, a worthwhile way to live out life'.

He relates that the harsh realities of growing up in a rough Irish school system where corporal punishment was thought to be the way to instil knowledge and wisdom in young pupils brought him close to understanding the experiences of physical abuse that many children still endure everyday in their homes and unforgiving societies. ' My schooldays were frequently filled with the dread and fear of mocking sarcastic teachers and brothers whose inner frustrations were vented on us hapless kids,' he said, 'The leather strap and swishing cane raised enough welts and seared memories that have given me a deep sense of compassion with all abused children and a healthy scepticism towards authority figures.'

'The poor, even when beaten down, falsely accused, tortured and deprived of everything, live on to survive with their dignity torn and tattered but intact. Jesus suffered the same. I find strength in him as I find him with the poor and want to help them, to be with them and take up their just cause. We have to be ready to endure what they suffer too.'

'Silence about abuse is consent,' he continues. 'I felt that to be honest with oneself, action is called for, not just talk and hand-wringing at how awful it is. I am a committed Christian, and I see this as a challenge as Jesus did.' His contribution has been recognised by many and he has been the recipient of numerous human rights awards. He received a German Human Rights of the City of Weimar Award in 2000, an Italian Human Rights Award at the City of Ferrara the following year, and was also nominated for the Nobel Peace Prize.

A few times it has felt hopeless to go on. 'So much evil, so much apathy here and abroad. But where else can I go? I know many people think that I am a dreamer, trying to change the world, but we have to try.'

Oftentimes a controversial figure, his stubborn streak and definitive refusal to accept the injustices of life give him strength. 'When I see the oppression and injustice in this world, the sea of poverty and the islands of glittering wealth and obscene extravagance floating among the bodies of the drowning, I feel something in me that says "don't accept this, don't turn away, don't ignore it and seek the easy life". They want me to back down,' he concludes. 'I won't.'

Bryan Dobson
Newsreader

As a child growing up in Sandymount, Bryan Dobson had a blissful and contented existence. He was a pupil of the nearby St Matthew's school and he remembers the pace of life in the early 1960s as leisurely and easygoing. 'I always remember the YMCA Sports Ground near our house,' he recalls. 'There was a big playground, cricket and tennis clubs – but I was never any good at sport!'

Now a highly experienced news anchor with RTÉ, away from the public eye Bryan maintains a keen interest in reading, business and politics, which have certainly been useful to him in obtaining the position he holds today. That position is a far cry from his first job as a teenager, assisting his father, a wine merchant. While the daily chore of this role was both mundane and tedious, the work did at least lead to the arrival of his first wage packet, and over twenty years later he can still recall his very first purchase from that pay packet. 'There was an electrical shop in Bachelors Walk and I bought one of those long-shaped tape recorders for ten pounds – they probably don't even make them any more!' Reminiscing, Dobson appreciates the freedom that he and his friends had growing up – more freedom than he and his wife would permit his own children, who are being raised in Portobello. 'We had the run of the place,' he recalls. 'I went everywhere on my bike, but my children have a good deal of freedom too. I wouldn't be paranoid about letting them out.'

He still takes great pleasure in exploring the streets of Dublin and observing the positive changes of city life, taking regular strolls along O'Connell Street and delighting in many of the inner city's most stately and scenic buildings. He takes particular pride in the modern Millennium Bridge along the quays, which was designed and constructed by a fellow Dubliner and friend.

Bemoaning the colossal increase in traffic and the lack of adequate parking facilities in the capital, he thinks 'the traffic could be managed better if they made a better job of public transport.' The whole subject of traffic stirs another memory – the purchase of his first car. 'A bright yellow monstrosity!' he says. 'I bought it in 1984 for £800 and I remember driving up to collect my wife, who was then my girlfriend, and she was mortified!'

But things have improved since then and the yellow car is but a distant memory. Following a stint as current affairs reporter with the BBC in Belfast, Dobson returned to Dublin and emerged over time as a familiar face on Irish television screens, reporting the news of many monumental events, including the European Summit at Dublin Castle, the devastation of famine-ridden Ethiopia and the fall of the Berlin Wall.

Despite his well-groomed and perfectly manicured appearance, Dobson says he will never forget those awkward teenage years. 'I went to my first disco in Wesley at the age of twelve or thirteen and had long hair. I wore flares, and cheesecloth shirts, which were in at the time. It was the seventies,' he says by way of explanation.

Ken Doherty

Snooker Player

In the early 1980s, a young lad from Ranelagh was, like many others, spending his spare time hanging around the local snooker hall and mixing with his peers. But there was something notably different about this lad. He displayed a rare and brilliant talent, which the owners of one establishment were quick to recognise and nurture. Today former Embassy World Snooker Champion Ken Doherty is back where it all began, although the circumstances in which I encountered him are a little different. Gone is the teenage boy who queued up to use the snooker table during school lunchtimes and in his place is a mature and accomplished superstar who lays claim to his own separate base upstairs in Jason's of Ranelagh – a room for a champion. Its centrepiece is a full-size snooker table and the walls are adorned with glossy framed photographs that capture the magic of those special moments – Ken beating Stephen Hendry in the 1997 World Championship, Ken meeting George Best, Ken challenging his childhood idol Alex Higgins to a game.

Staring in wonder at these images of his success, Doherty takes a sharp intake of breath, appearing genuinely mystified as he reflects on his own progression to international acclaim. Looking back on the sequence of events leading up to his career, it's not difficult to understand why he should feel such a close bond to the village in which he was raised. The greatest bond of all is to Jason's. For it was the owners of this now famous snooker club who backed Ken, and it is solely thanks to the unconditional investment of their time and generosity that he was given the opportunity to explore his full potential.

Born in Holles Street Hospital, Dublin, in 1969, one of a family of four, the young Ken attended Westland Row Christian Brothers School. It was during these early formative years that the first seeds of a glittering career were firmly planted. 'I was given my first snooker cue at the age of ten, but I wasn't allowed into Jason's, so I had to wait for my older brother to bring me on Sundays,' he recalls. 'There were loads of kids there, pool tables, space invaders machines – it was a cool place to be.'

Although the youngster was clearly becoming more accomplished with each game, as a thirteen-year-old schoolboy he could obviously ill afford to spend all his pocket money on the table, and this is where the intervention of the owners made a difference. 'They approached the manager, Andy Collins, who still works here, and agreed to give me free play every day; then they began to sponsor me in a local tournament, the Irish Under-Sixteen Senior League. Without their support, I would never have adapted or developed,' he says, deep gratitude plainly evident in his voice. From those amateur competitions and hours of disciplined practice, Ken Doherty, backed by his now escalating team of supporters, strove to make it into the highly competitive arena of professional snooker, a journey that was to see him leave behind the security of a close-knit community and venture out into the unknown.

Taking that first crucial step towards independence was a move recalled with a combination of honesty and affection. 'I moved to England where they had a quality system and it was hard,' he reveals. 'Homesickness, loneliness, the pressure of playing. You have to grow up very quickly. You learn about the washing machine and the fridge, and I learned how to change a plug!' From the isolation of his own flat and the major struggle in climbing in the rankings, the earnest Ken accepted a job at Goffs, a move that was to place him that little bit closer to his revered heroes. 'I worked in Goffs as an usher and it gave me a great insight. I got to meet all the players, and I always dreamt of being a great player.'

Yet the road to success was not uneventful. Along the way there were many obstacles and hurdles to overcome. 'Yes, I got frustrated,' he admits, momentarily reliving those difficult times again. 'Especially the year I didn't qualify for automatic professional status. I had to wait for another year. I threw my cue under the bed and said I never wanted to see it again!'

This brief interlude of disillusionment and despondency failed to seriously affect Doherty's fighting spirit, however, and he got back on track almost immediately, emerging victorious in the World Amateur Championship of 1989 and turning professional in 1990. 'But you do become very selfish, you develop tunnel vision,' he says. 'You know that you're representing your country and that everyone has such high expectations of you. It's down to you to make it.' Three years of intensive practice followed, during which he captured his first world ranking title (the 1993 Regal Welsh), and emerged a deserving member of an elite group that included the likes of Dennis Taylor, Stephen Hendry and Steve Davis. Of those numerous influential names and faces, one held particular significance. Since his boyhood years the high esteem in which he held this one man has never diminished. 'I loved Alex Higgins,' he proclaims, evidently still in awe of the man he always hoped to emulate. 'He was the best, so flamboyant, so charismatic and so unpredictable. I loved watching him play, he was a great entertainer.'

Without doubt Ken's greatest achievement to date remains the exhilarating Embassy World Snooker Championship victory of 1997, when he sailed home with an 18-12 victory against Stephen Hendry. It is something that is forever etched in his memory. 'I'll never forget it,' he says smiling. 'There was a huge street party and a real carnival atmosphere.' Since that momentous occasion, Doherty has been hard at work, immersed in his craft for up to eight hours a day, perfecting his skills and enjoying further success in a variety of tournaments. As he looks to the future, he knows that he will consistently figure in the final stages of tournaments. But it is the 'big one' he's clearly aiming for again. 'I can win it again,' he states determinedly. 'I believe I'm good enough.'

Yet in spite of the fame, the fortune and the stardom, there's no place quite like home, according to Ken, who simply wouldn't live anywhere else. 'I live in Dublin, it's always been home,' he says. 'It's the best place to live, my family and friends are here and I have a nice life. The economy is good, the food is good, the entertainment is good – and the Guinness is good!'

Ronnie Drew
_____ Singer

Ronnie Drew is a true Dubliner in every sense of the word. Born on 16 September 1934, in the south County Dublin suburb of Dún Laoghaire, Drew was one of a family of six and first discovered his love of music through the radio.

'Radio was limited and better than it is today. Today they play the music that is presented to them by huge recording companies. I used to listen to *Ballad Makers Saturday Night* and began to get interested. I remember hearing Dominic Behan singing 'Finnegans Wake' and identified with it because there was an urban feel to it and I liked the song.'

'I heard folk music from all over the world – Greece, Italy and Spain. So I bought a guitar off someone for two bob, went to Spain in 1955 and learned how to play flamenco. Then I began accompanying myself on songs and when Val Brown took me to a fleadh ceoil, I really got to know what Irish music was all about and became very much involved in it.'

'When I was on stage I used to tell a few stories, and then I joined John Molloy on stage in the Gate Theatre and used to tell a few gags in between singing songs.'

Soon the first steps towards the formation of The Dubliners were beginning to take shape. 'Myself and Barney McKenna teamed up and we'd go to O'Donoghue's pub where we met Luke Kelly and we used to sit there playing in a corner – and eventually somebody asked us to play a few gigs. Luke had just come back from England and brought a lot of songs with him and that broadened my horizons and I became interested in songs that had something to say.'

'We got a job in the Abbey Tavern in Howth playing every Saturday night but I came to the realisation that we were getting paid very little, so we went across the road to the Royal Hotel and spoke to Mr Gibley about playing there. He had a 1930s ballroom and we played to a full house every Saturday night for a year. Then Mick McCarthy opened up the Embankment and we played there and in the Grafton Cinema.'

The foursome made their debut performance in 1962 in O'Donoghue's Pub in Dublin's Merrion Row. They performed at the 1963 Edinburgh Festival and their 1967 rendition of 'Seven Drunken Nights' entered the UK Top Ten and led to an appearance on BBC TV's *Top of the Pops.*

Ronnie first left The Dubliners in 1974, then rejoined and finally departed in 1994. This was a major transition for him, and he went on to impress his loyal fans and critics alike with his album 'Dirty Rotten Shame'. He has enjoyed teaming up with the cream of Irish musical artists including Stockon's Wing, De Dannan, Eamonn Campbell, Eleanor Shanley, Donal Lunny, Antonio Breschi and the Hothouse Flowers.

To date there are over two hundred different collections of The Dubliners' music available, as well as solo albums by individual members of the group. Their LPs include 'A Drop of the Hard Stuff', 'Drunken and Courtin', 'At It Again,' 'Double Dubliners,' '21 Years On,' 'A Parcel of Rogues,' '30 Years a Greying,' and 'Alive Alive O!'.

In 1992 The Dubliners celebrated their thirtieth anniversary with a double CD and an extensive tour, and some twenty-five years after their first *Top of the Pops* performance, they appeared again, this time with Shane McGowan and The Pogues, singing 'The Irish Rover'.

Ronnie's 1997 stage production of 'Ronnie I Hardly Knew Ya', which he co-wrote with former Stockons Wing member Mike Hanrahan, also travelled to the 1998 Edinburgh Fringe Festival and as far afield as the USA, Denmark, Hungary, the Czech Republic and Israel. 'The one man show was hugely successful,' he says. People often equate success with money and I didn't make a lot of money, but it got fantastic reviews and was a project I had seen through successfully.'

Drew also appeared in Sean O'Casey's *Purple Dust* and in *Joseph and his Amazing Technicolor Dreamcoat* at the Gaiety. He partnered actor/comedian Niall Tóibín in *Bells of Hell* and teamed up with his son Phelim in the BBC production *The Ambassador*.

These days Ronnie seems somewhat disillusioned with the way Dublin has changed. 'All my old favourite places now have televisions and football and people roaring and young people who, in the main, seem to be unable to have conversations and just shout at each other and say "Deadly!" and "What's the Story?" and they're not really looking for a story at all. And the idea of almost having to show your passport to get into a pub puts me off as well, added to the fact that I don't drink. My favourite places were where you could once go, meet people of a similar outlook and have a conversation – and you'd at least be able to hear each other and stories would be told. Now you find there's a change in the language and all our old turns of phrase have gone. You have to speak a certain type of language and drink a special kind of beer and the stranger the name of the beer the more attractive it is, which leads me to believe that they don't have any real taste.'

He is also quite critical of contemporary music. 'Young people's taste in music seems to be foisted upon them and not something that they have nurtured themselves. When I was young I listened to the radio and formulated my own tastes. I liked jazz, I liked blues, I liked a broad spectrum of music and now young people in a general way seem to only go for whatever the market tells them. The market will tell them what they want and individuality seems to be a thing of the past. When I think of manufactured bands, if I think of them at all, I think of a complete lack of imagination. At least we played our own instruments and sang our own songs.'

Frank Duff

Co-Founder of the
Legion of Mary

Frank Duff was born and bred in St Patrick's Road, Drumcondra. He attended the Little Dame School as a young boy and in later years Belvedere and Blackrock College. A warm and likeable young man, he proved to be a highly competent and proficient pupil. His caring demeanor was evident in his decision to forfeit his plans for a university education, however, in order to help his family make ends meet after his father had to retire early due to ill health.

Frank began his career as a civil servant with the Land Commission, and later moved to both the Department of Finance and the Department of Agriculture. Despite this rise up the career ladder and the obvious potential for material and financial gain, he remained deeply concerned by the plight of the city's under-privileged citizens and vowed to make his contribution.

He did this by joining the Society of St Vincent de Paul in 1914. In the course of his charity work he came into close contact with social problems – widespread unemployment, high crime and deep depression. Affected by the sheer futility of the situation and resolving to make a difference, Frank Duff enlisted the support of his pal Matt Lalor and together they founded the Legion of Mary in 1921.

This move generated a mixed response, not least from the church – the then Archbishop of Dublin viewed the lay organisation with much scepticism and refused to give the church's approval to the society's handbook. The acceptance of the church was not achieved until the early 1950s. But such obstacles were not enough to suppress Duff and Lalor's deep-rooted commitment to those less fortunate, and the Legion grew and prospered at a rapid rate, devoting itself to voluntary apostolic and charity work.

In 1928 Frank Duff reaffirmed his commitment to Dublin's poor, and brought into existence the Morning Star Hostel in the city centre, which became a sanctuary for the homeless, the starving and the forgotten. It provided a haven for those who desperately needed rescuing from the harsh realities of the time – unmarried mothers, victims of abuse and innocent children born into frightful circumstances.

The society later switched its Dublin base to Scotland and established similar branches in places as far away as Australia, Asia and Africa. It incorporated prison and hospital visits and round-the-clock care for the poor, the abandoned and the destitute – a remarkable testament to the sympathetic heart and human compassion of one Irishman.

Throughout many years of active association with the Legion of Mary, Frank continued his work in the civil service and found time to record his thoughts in *The Legion of Mary Handbook, Walking with Mary* and *Mary Shall Reign*. His writings brought to light his obvious devotion to Our Lady, a major motivational factor in the continuance of his selfless deeds.

Frank Duff retired in 1933 and presided over the establishment of additional units of a now worldwide organisation. His unfailing enthusiasm and generous nature were acknowledged through the presentation of the Papal Order of St Gregory the Great, and he was granted an honorary LL.D. from the National University of Ireland.

Throughout a long and active life, Frank Duff kept up his commitment to the poor. He died in his own hostel, the Morning Star, in 1980, at the age of ninety-one.

Joe Duffy

Broadcaster

Joe Duffy, who was born in Mountjoy Square in 1956, spend most of his early childhood in Ballyfermot and is proud of his Dublin heritage. It's been an interesting transformation from social worker to broadcaster and producer but he strongly believes his previous occupation was an advantage when it came to breaking the second. 'I became a social worker for a reason – because I was interested in working with people and helping them; the same compulsion actually works to your advantage in radio,' says the man who displays an extraordinary skill for communicating with people and putting them at their ease.

So what's his secret? 'Well, I think if you're a good listener and if you do actually care … I don't believe for one minute that I'm any more intelligent than the next person. It helps when you listen to people. Everyone's story is genuine.' The 'stories' he refers to of course are those heard daily on the RTÉ Radio *Liveline* programme, which Joe has made his own since Marian Finucane vacated the chair in 1998.

Joe's Dublin wit and easy rapport with his audience is obvious. 'Well, I seem to have a knack with my audience,' he admits. 'It's where I work best, interacting with people on a one-to-one level. In most of the successful television shows – Cilla Black, Noel Edmonds – the main ingredient is a live audience and I must say that appeals to me.'

Now in his fourth year as host, Joe says he 'loves the programme and don't know when it will ever end!' He is clearly contented and comfortable with both the respect and the responsibility that comes with the job – but like most broadcasters he has had his fair share of criticism. 'The one thing I don't do with criticism is dismiss it. Everyone has a valid point of view; you listen to it, but you have to get the balance right.'

Joe and his wife June have their hands full with their young triplets Ronan, Sean and Ellen and have no reservations about bringing them up in a city which has altered dramatically over the years – and not always for the better. 'Dublin is busier now, which is great,' he muses 'and there are more nationalities, which is also positive. But the collapsing infrastructure needs to be addressed urgently,' he adds. Looking back, the Ballyfermot native has come a long way. 'But it was still a big gamble from a permanent pensionable job in the civil service to a contract job in RTÉ – I could have been gone in six months!' he laughs with the easy confidence of a man who has achieved his ambition.

Robert Emmet
Patriot

Affectionately known as 'the darlin' of Erin', Robert Emmet was born in 1778 in St Stephen's Green, Dublin, one of a family of seventeen and the son of Dr and Mrs Robert Emmet.

He attended Samuel Whyte's Academy in Grafton Street and then Trinity College, where he was to meet and befriend Thomas Moore and Richard Curran. Clearly following in the footsteps of and sharing the same political ambitions as his elder brother Thomas, he became an enthusiastic member of the United Irishmen. Thomas was arrested in March 1798 and, in a search for United Irishmen among the student body, Robert's name was removed from the list of undergraduates.

From 1800 until 1802 Emmet travelled around the Continent, meeting United Irishmen and the French in an effort to plan a fresh insurrection against the British with the support of the French. Following an unsatisfactory meeting with Napoleon, Emmet returned to Dublin in October 1802.

Back at home, he sought refuge in his father's house while ammunition was gathered and stored in Dublin, but a year later an explosion at one of his arms depots led him to bring forward his plans, and he called for a rising on July 23. This was doomed from the start – the Wicklow contingent never turned up and the Kildare men mistakenly thought the rising had been postponed. While on a march against Dublin Castle, Emmet's party attacked and killed the lord chief justice, Lord Kilwarden, and his nephew, who were unfortunate enough to encounter him.

Realising the potential consequences of his actions and fearing imminent capture, Emmet maintained a low profile by hiding in a hut in Mount Drummond Avenue, Harold's Cross, in the aftermath of the aborted rebellion.

Adding further drama to Emmet's tragic story is his love affair with Sarah Curran which began in autumn 1802. Although her father disapproved of the relationship, the couple were able to keep in regular contact and wrote letters to each other. After the rising Emmet refused to leave Dublin, wanting to be near Sarah, despite the danger this decision meant for his personal safety.

He was eventually captured and charged. The acclaimed lawyer John Philpot Curran, Sarah's father, who had previously defended Wolfe Tone and Rowan Hamilton, refused to defend him. Emmet's speech from the dock (although some of this was not actually spoken by him), is regarded as one of Ireland's classical political texts:

'Let my memory be left in oblivion and my tomb remain uninscribed until other times and other men can do justice to my character. When my country takes her place among the nations of the earth, then and not till then, let my epitaph be written.'

To be forever hailed as a hero, Robert Emmet was tried for treason and subsequently hanged on 20 September 1803, leaving Sarah heartbroken. She married in 1805, but never recovered from the death of her beloved Emmet.

In a way neither did Ireland, where today there stands a statue opposite the site of the now demolished house where he was born.

Colin Farrell
Actor

It's a long way from Ballykissangel to Hollywood and it's been a rollercoaster ride for one of Dublin's most promising actors. The young and handsome Colin Farrell has hit the big time in spectacular style and it all dates back to early childhood when the young man from Castleknock saw his sister win a part in *A Midsummer Night's Dream* at the Gaiety School of Acting and was bitten by the drama bug.

'Catherine and I, more than any of the others, were always into the movies, staying up late as kids watching the old Hollywood black-and-whites,' he told *Irish America* magazine.

As a teenager, he chose to become an actor rather than follow in the footsteps of his father Eamon Farrell, and his uncle, Tommy, who both played for Shamrock Rovers at the height of their success. Some thirty thousand fans watched them beat Red Star Belgrade in 1961.

Colin attended school in Castleknock for three years, before moving on to Gormanstown and Bruce College. There followed a year out in Australia where he made his stage debut in a play based on the life of outlaw Ned Kelly. 'The play was terrible but it was the first time I'd rehearsed with a bunch of actors. And once back in Dublin I decided to give acting a go.' He made his European stage debut playing a teenage autistic boy in *In a Little World of Our Own* by Gary Mitchell at London's Donmar Warehouse. Following a period as a student at the Gaiety School of Drama, Farrell won the part of Danny in *Ballykissangel*, followed by parts in Deirdre Purcell's *Falling for a Dancer*, and with Kevin Spacey in *Ordinary Decent Criminal*, the film based on the life of Dublin gangster Martin Cahill.

But it was his portrayal of Bozz in *Tigerland* that made him a household name in Hollywood and for which he garnered a Best Actor Award from the Boston Society of Film Critics. Ironically it was a role which may never have seen the light of day but for the intervention of his sister who has always been an invaluable support to him. Catherine filmed her brother in action at his Irishtown flat. 'She's very good with a camcorder,' he says. 'It was the most crucial few minutes I'll probably ever do on film.'

It was certainly an audition that greatly impressed film director Joel Schumacher, who said of that time, 'Colin just filled the room with humour and charm and I decided to have him read for the lead in *Tigerland*. He reminded me of Paul Newman in *Cool Hand Luke*, or Jack Nicholson in *One Flew Over the Cuckoo's Nest*.'

As Danny in *Ballykissangel*, Colin was used to working with horses but the open fields of Avoca, Co Wicklow were nothing compared to the challenges which faced him when he joined the cast of the romantic action adventure film *American Outlaws* to play the legendary Jesse James. 'I'd done a bit of bare-back riding when I was playing Danny but nothing like this. All I had to do in *Ballykissangel* was trot two yards, get into the shot and get off. *American Outlaws* was the real stuff.'

Despite being part of the glitz and glamour of Hollywood, Colin remains true to his Irish roots and still has his flat near Sandymount strand in Dublin. 'There are a few nice pubs around the corner, and a chipper,' he says. 'That's all I need. I don't have a toothbrush or a pair of slippers in LA.'

'I've been lucky,' says Colin, who recently starred alongside Bruce Willis in *Hart's War*. 'I've skipped about 100 rungs on the ladder. So I don't have to go and live in LA or do the scene there to get noticed. I can go there, do the work and get out. I'm in no hurry to get anywhere. I don't have any plans. I don't have a map. If you did in this business, you'd destroy yourself. Those who don't know me might think I've turned arrogant, but I don't think I have. If it's all taken away from me tomorrow I have a family and friends that I love and I'll find something else to do.'

Barry Fitzgerald
Actor

Among the many great stars of stage and screen to emerge out of Ireland, one pair of talented brothers achieved immense fame and recognition in a relatively short period of time. William Joseph (later Barry Fitzgerald) and Arthur Shields were born at Walworth Road, Portobello, and attended Green Lane National School and later Merchant's Tailor School.

Arthur displayed a great love for drama early on and was soon treading the boards of Dublin's Abbey Theatre. By 1914 he had made the decision to pursue acting as a serious profession and got parts in *The Playboy of the Western World* and *Shadow and Substance* amongst many others, playing over a hundred different roles in all. He later left Dublin and headed for Hollywood, the place to be for an aspiring actor.

Meanwhile, back home in Dublin, his younger brother was embarking on a similar path and became a part-time actor in the Abbey, while holding a day-job as a civil servant. In later years William Joseph Shields changed his name to Barry Fitzgerald – a name that was to travel far and wide and become one in a long line of established and highly regarded names in the theatrical and film world.

Showing great promise, even in his early years, Barry was instrumental in shaping one of the principal characters in Sean O'Casey's *Juno and the Paycock*, achieving further success with *The Plough and the Stars*, another O'Casey production, apparently written especially with Fitzgerald in mind.

Due to the controversial content of this drama, it generated fierce publicity and even threats of abduction, so the young actor maintained a low profile and went on to embrace other roles, generally being cast in comic drama and invariably causing pandemonium. Fitzgerald could depict the mischievous imp brilliantly and with tremendous bursts of energy.

Despite establishing a reputation for himself and not just as 'Arthur Shields' younger brother', Barry yearned for the serious roles his elder brother undertook and he too set sail for the bright lights of Hollywood, going on to feature in over forty-five films. He won an Oscar for his part in *Going My Way* alongside Bing Crosby, and he also performed with screen legends John Wayne and Maureen O'Hara in *The Quiet Man*.

The two brothers exhibited a wonderful and phenomenal respect for their trade, bringing real life and authenticy to each and every role. They were buried alongside one another in Deansgrange cemetery.

Brendan Grace
Comedian

One of Ireland's best-loved ambassadors of comedy and music, Brendan Grace is celebrating over thirty years in showbusiness. Having 'conquered' Ireland many years ago, he is now growing in popularity in the United States, and divides his time between his sunny Florida home and his native Dublin, where he regularly appears on television and in cabaret.

Grace has affectionate memories of how it all began. 'I have an aunt, Wyn Meyler, who now lives in South Carolina. She was a very famous model in Ireland when I was young and I was always impressed that every hotel porter and taxi driver seemed to know her. She used to take me to the Gresham Hotel for tea and I was very impressed by the life she led and it probably gave me a taste of the good life. I also worked in my uncle's pub on Wexford Street (now The Mean Fiddler), in the early 1960s. It was a singing pub and I used to sing a couple of songs like 'Ghost Riders in the Sky' and 'Lovely Leitrim'. I wasn't paid, but that didn't matter. Singing in the pub and seeing my aunt being recognised were probably the two most important things that encouraged me to go into showbusiness.'

Brendan began his professional career as a singer with the Gingermen prior to emigrating to Canada in 1971 to pursue solo work. His natural delivery and comic flair shone through his act and he went on to become one of Ireland's most successful comedians. He created the lovable rogue 'Bottler', and his own composition 'Combine Harvester' reached number one in the charts in 1980.

Brendan spent his first professional wage packet on an engagement ring for his girlfriend, Eileen, now his wife of twenty-eight years, with whom he lives in Palm Beach, Florida, along with the couple's four children, Amanda, Melanie, Bradley and Brendan Patrick. He has performed in Carnegie Hall, Radio City, Westbury Music Fair, London's Theatre Hall, New London Arena and Sydney Festival Theatre. He also appeared with fellow Dubliner, the late Dermot Morgan, in Channel Four's *Father Ted* and has produced numerous audio and videotapes along the way.

In 1991 Grace, now established as one of Ireland's top comedians, was asked to entertain musical legends Frank Sinatra, Sammy Davis Junior and Liza Minnelli at a private function in Dublin. The response from 'Ol Blue Eyes' was more than favourable and led to an offer of secure work in the US for Grace. With a young family to consider, the decision to emigrate was not taken lightly. 'When we went, we decided to try it for two years at the most. It was a case of just going and seeing what would happen. Now we absolutely adore living here, with the weather and the way of life. But Ireland is and will always be home.'

Three decades on from his first days on stage, Brendan enjoys sell-out runs in Dublin's Gaiety Theatre. And appearing before a live audience has always been important to him. 'I was the person who stepped into Jack Cruise's shoes at the Olympia Theatre after his death. He was a hard act to follow, but I did it. I would like to acknowledge the fact that people like Jack Cruise, Cecil Sheridan, Maureen Potter, Danny Cummins, Chris Casey and Val Fitzpatrick are all the people I tried to emulate when I went into the theatre. They were the people who influenced me the most.'

Coming home and seeing the response of the Irish was clearly very special to him. 'To receive a standing ovation every night was really more important than money. Words cannot describe the feeling you get when a packed theatre stands on its feet. It was very emotional. Being a Dub, I used to close with 'Dublin in the Rare Auld Times', but some nights I had to let the audience sing it. I just couldn't. I had to hold myself back from breaking down. Without a doubt that was the highlight of my career.'

Tony Gregory
Politician

'I was pretty wild,' admits Tony Gregory TD about his schooldays, 'but it wasn't earth-shattering stuff! I robbed orchards and we used to scuttle on the grain lorries! I remember the great excitement when I saw Sheriff Street for the first time – I jumped off one of the lorries and saw all these huge blocks of flats! I didn't rob cars or anything, because there weren't any to rob, but if there were, I might have!'

Born in Charleville Avenue, off the North Strand, this highly respected public representative had a colourful and eventful early life in terms of his education. He first attended the Loreto Convent in North Great George's Street, at the age of three. It was labeled 'Hill Street' because pupils entered the school by the back gate of a yard leading on to Hill Street. The earnest scholar later went to St Cannon's Christian Brothers school, on Dublin's North Circular Road, which had just introduced a unique venture known as a 'corporation scholarship', specifically aimed at catering for children from the outer suburbs. Those typical inner city schooldays were, according to Tony, 'not particularly unhappy, but tough'. Tough seems a mild description, given the extent to which corporal punishment was used at the time. 'I remember the severe hidings on my hands and knuckles from the Christian Brothers. I remember playing on the fire escape at break time and I threw a banger which exploded and got a great cheer from the assembled crowd! Then the Head brother, nicknamed 'Fish Face', because his name was Herring, threatened to beat the shit out of everyone if the culprit didn't own up, so myself and another lad owned up and he beat us on the knuckles with a round pointed stick.'

Emerging as a bit of a rebel, the youthful Tony was nonetheless a sensitive soul who was forced to deal with a wide range of emotions throughout his adolescence, partially in light of the fact that his mother suffered from TB, ensuring unpredictable periods of illness for her, fuelled by constant anxieties about the future. 'It was hard, and an unhappy time,' he admits. 'We were always worried about her going into hospital and maybe losing her,' he says, his voice trailing off in sorrow.

In later years, Tony achieved degrees in history and Irish in UCD and embarked upon a teaching career, while maintaining a keen interest in local politics. He was heavily swayed by the views of his father, who continually related stories of historical and political events such as the 1916 Rising and the Black and Tans years. 'My father was a great admirer of Michael Collins and hated de Valera, while the rest of the country admired de Valera and hated Collins! But he was a big influence,' he says, 'and when you spend twelve years of your life in one room, with no running water, no toilet, it's bound to have an effect – you become interested in equality in Ireland and the difference between those who have and those who have not.'

Tony Gregory initiated his first political campaign in 1979 and worked intimately with community associations in the north inner city. He was elected to the Dáil in 1982 as an independent TD. He involved himself in a long line of significant issues, thereby firmly establishing his standing as a man of the people. He became the voice of the downtrodden and underprivileged, delivering much for the inner city through the famous 'Gregory deal', hatched with then Taoiseach Charles Haughey, in return for the independent TD's support for a Fianna Fáil government. 'I focus on what other politicians don't,' he states confidently. 'I represent the people who are demanding support and aren't getting it, things that had a devastating effect on the area – the plight of the Moore Street Women Traders; animal cases; areas the mainstream politicians find too awkward.'

So what of Dublin, the city of his birth? 'The north inner city is in the process of continual change; housing conditions have changed dramatically from the overcrowded tenement areas. The transformation of the North Wall and the financial services centre – it's a world away from what I grew up with.' This consistently re-elected TD, whose work covers such areas as the inner city to Castleknock, maintains a deep fondness for the old traditional parts of Dublin – with one area in particular transporting him right back to childhood. 'I've always had an attraction for Henry Street at Christmas,' he smiles. 'The trees, the lights and the stars were incredible and I can never understand how the city council and big stores wanted to get rid of that. It is part of the catalyst that attracts people. It's also where the struggle of the Moore Street traders took place and where my mother did her shopping – it's a part of Dublin,' he says.

This round-the-clock campaigner deals with an extensive amount of daily requests, both from his Leinster House office and advice centres located throughout the city. For Tony Gregory, one staunch crusader of the past remains a source of deep inspiration: 'Noel Browne – for a number of reasons. His parents died of TB, and my mother died of TB. He became Minister for Health and crusaded on social issues. I would never aspire to compare myself to him but I admire him greatly.'

Unfortunately, in spite of the great advances of the last few decades, one issue of major concern remains the horrific plague of drug abuse. 'I don't think the answer is to build more treatment centres,' he says. 'It's a bit late in the day for that, although they are obviously a necessity. The main problem is social disadvantage and social inequality. Until we get to the stage where we create a more just society, treat all the children of the nation equally, and oppose the ready availability of drugs, we won't progress. If we get equality, people will be less likely to want to destroy themselves with escapist drugs.' Some may view this as an unrealistic 'pie in the sky' dream but it's an admirable goal to aim for. Should it materialise, this man will surely have played a contributory role.

Arthur Guinness

Brewer

It's difficult to know where to begin when attempting to analyse the success of Dublin's most famous asset – Guinness. Who could have known that one man's genius would see this drink become one of Ireland's most famous exports and an institution in itself?

The company's first premises was in Leixlip, Co Kildare. A move to Dublin was facilitated by the generosity of one Dr Price, Archbishop of Cashel, whose legacy of £100 helped finance the impressive and spacious James's Gate Brewery, an ideal location close to the city's water supply. Arthur and his wife, Olivia Whitmore, moved to Thomas Street in Dublin. Despite initial attempts at brewing a number of very different beverages, Arthur Guinness recognised the unique taste and strong potential of porter (named after the porters at London's Convent Garden market). Guinness, officially defined as 'a heavy black top fermented beer', was first brewed in 1778, and was to lead to unimagined success for the Guinness family. Arthur and his wife had twenty-one children in all, but only ten survived to adulthood. They were to benefit greatly from the ambitious streak and business sense of their father.

Although most small towns had their own breweries, Arthur Guinness recognised a gap in the market and set about distributing Guinness to public houses around Ireland, using the barges along Ireland's canals.

Success brought its own problems, however, and Arthur faced allegations from Dublin Corporation of taking more water for brewing than he was freely entitled to, in addition to the added complication of a government tax being placed on brewers' products in a bid to raise revenue. A heated debate on the issue followed in the Irish House of Commons. Gaining support from Henry Grattan, a relative of his wife, Arthur Guinness succeeded in getting the tax on beer abolished.

A man of the people, Arthur was known as a kindly and selfless man who was responsive to the needs of his employees. He donated a significant amount of his wealth to St Patrick's Cathedral, The Moyne Institute for medical research and the headquarters of the Department of Foreign Affairs. He was also responsible for the establishment of a large house in Whitehall, which was to be transformed into a convalescent home following his death in 1803.

Today Guinness' brewery represents an integral part of Dublin's culture and heritage, attracting a steady stream of visitors.

The Guinness dynasty is one of the largest in Europe and the biggest exporter of stout in the world. Arthur Guinness lies in a vault near Kill in Co Kildare, and whether in Berlin, Paris, Rome or New York, the name lives on and stands as undoubtedly Ireland's greatest success story to date. Cheers!

Tom Hyland

East Timor Campaigner

Just over ten years ago, Tom Hyland, like so many others, was blissfully unaware of the existence of East Timor or the horrors of day-to-day life there. But all that changed with a revealing and hard-hitting television documentary, which showed graphic illustrations of the hardships experienced by the East Timorese. Deeply struck by these disturbing images, Tom resigned from a reliable post with Dublin Bus and started a campaign to aid the needy of that country. When questioned as to what actually drove him to take such a risk and embark on this unpredictable and potentially dangerous mission, he answers with a weary sigh, 'The sheer injustice of it all, the sheer injustice.'

Today Tom is in his Dame Street office, a blur of activity against a background of stark campaign posters, press releases and haunting photographic images. It's clear that this man and the group he single-handedly established have come a long way since those early tentative days. 'We made phone calls from public phone boxes which swallowed up our fifty-pence pieces!' he says with a grin, 'and we got the 78A bus into Fleet Street, knocking on doors and offices looking for a typewriter.' With donations from various businesses around Dublin they eventually succeeded in obtaining what was needed to kick-start their campaign.

From this base, phone calls are frantically made, faxes sent, letters posted. To whom? 'To anyone who will listen,' replies Tom. Irish people, he believes, have a duty to respond to the pleas of these victims, wretched people with haunted eyes and heavy hearts. However, this soft-spoken man claims to have seen a noticeable and negative change in society's attitude. 'Things are changing — with the Celtic Tiger I see an arrogance of affluence and people are pulling away. Everything we've been told about in relation to common decency has been turned on its head in relation to East Timor and it is simply not acceptable,' he says defiantly.

Hyland's experiences and memories of the place he strives to help have not been without drama. He was arrested on one occasion, but despite some horrific and distressing memories he is both unwilling and unable to let go, to desert the people to whom he has literally become a saviour. Graphic descriptions of incidents etched forever in his mind serve as a constant motivating factor and a stark reminder that this is no bleak paperback novel. 'For over twenty-three years these people have been brutalised and traumatised and have never been given any support from the outside world, and I think it is one of the greatest crimes of this century, where people have been abandoned. I still reel in horror when I talk to the Timorese or reflect on some of the stories … and it wears you down, emotionally, physically and mentally.'

Despite these demands and pressures, Tom Hyland displays an admirable determination to continue the battle. 'We can talk about figures and statistics, but these people are all individuals and human beings who are suffering. They could have been good or bad people, but they have a right to live their lives and nobody has a right to take that away.'

James Joyce
Writer

Labelled as quite possibly the twentieth century's greatest and most influential writer, James Augustine Aloysius Joyce was born in 1882 in Brighton Square, Rathgar, the eldest child in a middle-class family. His father, John Joyce (described by Joyce's distinguished biographer, Richard Ellmann, as the 'most gifted reprobate in Ireland'), enjoyed the benefits of an enviable financial status until he lost it all through his addiction to alcohol and the subsequent loss of his job as a tax collector. As the money began to disappear, so too did the luxurious lifestyle that James was accustomed to. The Joyces were forced to leave the southside of Dublin and move to the poverty-stricken north inner city. Ironically, it was this environment that fuelled James Joyce's imagination. The young James was forced to leave Clongowes, his beloved Jesuit school, but a chance encounter between his father and the then headmaster of Mountjoy Square's Belvedere College, Fr Conmee SJ, offered fresh hope and James and two of his brothers were offered free education.

He remained there until 1898 when he attended another Jesuit institution, the

Catholic University (now University College, Dublin), where he excelled at languages and music. At one stage he even considered the spiritual life of the priesthood. But on reflection, this would surely have been a disastrous choice, given the obvious limitations it would have had on his sexual life — at the age of fourteen, Joyce had his first of many encounters with prostitutes.

In 1902, when he was twenty, Joyce travelled to Paris with the intention of studying medicine. However, it was not to be and in 1904 he returned home to Dublin on the death of his mother and began writing seriously, producing *epicleti* which later became the book of poetry titled *Epiphanies*. But 1904 is notable for another reason – Joyce's first meeting with his future partner Nora Barnacle (they didn't get married until some twenty years later). Although the couple may have appeared on the surface as a somewhat unlikely pairing, they survived on a comfortable rather than a passionate level and raised two children, Giorgio and Lucia. They left Dublin in October 1904 and travelled throughout Europe, an unsurprising course of action, given the writer's hostility towards the land of his birth. Claiming it both infuriated and crippled him, he went so far as to describe its citizens as the 'most hopeless, useless and inconsistent race of characters' he had ever come across. This love-hate relationship with Ireland had a positive side and provided Joyce's inspiration for *Dubliners*, published in 1914, followed by *A Portrait of the Artist as a Young Man*.

Ulysses, the novel that eventually secured Joyce's reputation as a writer, was published in Paris in 1922. Set in Dublin, the story follows a day in the life of an eccentric couple. Introducing readers to a bizarre array of characters, Joyce's 'stream of consciousness' style of writing revolutionised the novel form.

He spent almost twenty years working on his next novel, *Finnegans Wake*. Failing eyesight hampered him and he also struggled with personal difficulties, such as the mental instability of his daughter, diagnosed by C. G. Jung as schizophrenic. *Finnegans Wake* was finally published in 1939. It stands as one of his most impressive pieces of work and the subject of positive criticism by many, including Samuel Beckett.

Joyce died in 1941 following complications after surgery for a stomach ulcer and was laid to rest in Zurich, the place he had eloped to with Nora a few months after they met. He wrote his own epitaph, which summed up his mixed sentiments towards his city. He said that when he died, the word 'Dublin' would be found engraved upon his heart.

Frank Kelly
Actor

A veteran of stage and screen, Frank Kelly is one of Ireland's most renowned actors. Having started in the Abbey Theatre and gone on to a career in England, the Dublin native has now returned to his home city.

Born and raised in Blackrock and educated at Blackrock College, Kelly gives great credit to his devoted parents for the environment in which he and his siblings were raised and nurtured. 'It was a very liberal home,' he reflects. 'There was lots of discussion and a great emphasis on self-worth and self-importance. We lived in a very interesting district.'

Following his early education, Frank attended University College, Dublin, studying law and exploring a great love for drama, which subsequently led to his becoming 'deeply immersed in the Old Eblana Theatre'. Despite having to combine this newfound interest with his legal studies, he revealed a natural talent for performing and later turned professional, beginning a lengthy and successful career. It's a career that has seen inspired performances in stand-up comedy sketches and straight acting.

The Kelly family spent their holidays in rural Ireland, County Clare in particular: 'I used to go down to the woods and pick blackberries. It was very pleasant and full of basic innocence. All those roads are built on now. It's all different,' he says sadly. 'We also used to go out on the farm. There were so many playgrounds and wide open spaces. I was born at a time when there was no transport, there were horses and carts and no cars, no petrol. You forget how different it all was.' Of his student days he recalls: 'Dublin was where I spent my time, had my love affairs and was at the heart of the action.'

Frank Kelly made his name in Ireland through his long-running starring roles in the satirical TV show *Hall's Pictorial Weekly*, the brainchild of the late Frank Hall, a weekly television feast which was the bane of politicians. It was a massive success in the 1970s and Kelly's hilarious contributions are fondly remembered.

A great deal of Kelly's working life was spent in England, where in recent times he memorably portrayed the irrepressible and not very endearing Father Jack, alongside Ardal O'Hanlon, Pauline McGlynn and the late Dermot Morgan, in the award-winning Channel Four comedy *Father Ted*. 'England was different but I was treated very well and well paid,' he says.

Now this Dubliner is glad to be back in his home city, although he notes: 'Dublin has changed – there was always a close sense of community, but that is disappearing now. It has become more aggressive,' he says. 'But I see great hope too,' he adds, good-humouredly, 'signs of individualism and less conformity. It's still better than most rural places!'

Luke Kelly

Singer

Forever associated with The Dubliners, Luke Kelly was one of Ireland's most revered entertainers during an all-too-short lifetime. His powerful renditions of 'Raglan Road' and Phil Coulter's 'Scorn Not His Simplicity', to name but two of his songs, have stood the test of time.

Luke Kelly was born in 1940 in Lattimore Cottages, Sheriff Street. His family later moved to Whitehall in the city. An energetic youngster, he excelled in both sport and music, idolising the musical heroes of the day and aspiring from a young age to follow in their footsteps. In adulthood he became a performer and was soon earning rave reviews. He made his name playing to appreciative audiences in the clubs and pubs of England. On his return home to Dublin, Luke met up with Ronnie Drew and soon the wonderful combination that was the Dubliners was born.

The group went on to earn international acclaim, and local sessions in their hometown were followed by performances in front of vast audiences in cities such as London and New York. The crack, humour and porter associated with their hometown were vital ingredients in their concerts. At the peak of their success they were the epitome of many things Irish.

For their brightest star, however, the rewards of such success were not destined to last. The long hours and the lure of alcohol became too much for Luke Kelly and his health began to fail rapidly. Following the diagnosis of a brain tumour and subsequent operations, he eventually lost his fight for life in 1984. At just forty-three years of age, Luke Kelly died, leaving millions of fans grieving for a remarkable singer.

In honour of his unique spirit, courage and unrivalled talent, Dublin City dedicated Ballybough Bridge over the Tolka to the memory of Luke Kelly.

Adrian Kennedy
Broadcaster

'If you have something to say, say it to Adrian Kennedy.' A loud, defiant statement, a little like the loud, defiant conversation of those who phone in to Adrian Kennedy's late-night talk radio show on Dublin's FM 104. No subject is taboo between the hours of 10 pm and 1 am each weeknight, when you're likely to hear a wide range of topics discussed and debated, from pornography to drugs to neighbours from hell.

Never have the airwaves been so accessible to the ordinary Joe Soap, and quite rightly so, according to the man behind the microphone: 'I make no apologies for the people on my show. Just because they're not all from Dublin 4 or may not be very articulate doesn't mean they're not entitled to their point of view, and I hate the patronising view of some members of the media who describe them as the lowest common denominators,' he says.

Born in Upton Park, Ballybrack, Kennedy was a pupil of St John's Secondary School and later of Merrion College. His schooldays were at times traumatic, due to personal experiences of bullying which, ironically, led him to relate more easily to his listeners. 'I didn't enjoy school,' he admits candidly. 'I more or less just went and got through it but never said anything about the bullying – that's the way things were at the time.'

As a teenager Kennedy spent lengthy periods practising being a DJ. He got his first big breakthrough on East Coast Radio, as host of a morning talk show, and in 1994 he joined FM 104. His ability as a late-night jock was first realised when, as a stand-in for another presenter, he made the show his own.

Adrian confesses to feeling slightly wary and uncomfortable in his live shows. With debates on such potentially emotive topics as drink-driving and racism, his shows can lead to hostility and volatile outbursts. 'They can be very intimidating,' he readily concedes. 'I find them hard, even though they were my idea in the first place!'

The content of his programme is largely dictated by the massive influx of telephone calls and messages to a twenty-four-hour answering machine. In addition, a steady stream of correspondence and e-mails on a wide variety of topics demands an immediate response.

Undoubtedly one of the attractions of being a late-night radio show host is what Kennedy calls the 'anonymity' of the job. He understood the benefit of this one night driving home after a particularly heated show, which painted taxi drivers in a bad light. An overheard comment from one aggrieved member of the profession ran, 'If I get my hands on that Adrian Kennedy, I'll bleedin' kill him!'

Pat Kenny

Broadcaster

It was clear from early on that Pat Kenny was going to go a long way, and it is perhaps unsurprising that he became a prominent figure in Irish broadcasting. Born in Dublin's national maternity hospital, the young Pat grew up on the northside of the city, close to the Phoenix Park, where his father held the novel job of caretaker of Dublin Zoo! 'We didn't have a huge back yard, we had the Phoenix Park as our playground!' he laughs.

Fuelled by the hard graft of his father and the encouragement of his mother, he says he was 'an inveterate thinker' with an inquisitive mind. He studied engineering at UCD, but it was broadcasting that was eventually to win his affections. 'As children we were avid radio listeners,' says Pat, who was the only boy in a family of three. 'We listened to everything and we went to shows. We went to *Question Time* in the Phoenix Hall. It was just one of those things we did as a family.'

Kenny began his career as a full-time lecturer in Bolton Street College of Technology, teaching chemistry to architects and thermodynamics to motor engineers. In the early 1970s, he was chosen from four hundred applicants for a job in RTÉ. As an ambitious young journalist determined to make his mark, he rose to the challenge of his new role, both behind the scenes and in front of the camera on the current affairs programme *Today Tonight*, as well as in the newsroom, a period not unblemished by mishaps, as he sheepishly recalls. 'I remember trying to read the news with a frog in my throat, but I realise now that the audience at home thought this was a hoot! Audiences love disasters and I've had my fair share,' he laughs.

A variety of radio and television programmes were to follow, ranging from light entertainment to hard-hitting current affairs, *Kenny Live* to *Today with Pat Kenny*. When Gay Byrne retired as host of *The Late Late Show*, Kenny proved to be the maestro's successor.

At his best on a one-to-one basis, Pat takes a very serious and intensive approach to his work, emphasising the need for research on the subject. 'Try to know what the person is going to say so that if they say something dramatically different, you will recognise that as a surprise. Recognise it as something that should be followed. You know you can predict an interview reasonably well and then suddenly if they don't say what you expect, you know you have something that is fundamentally interesting. So research, research, research is the basis of it all.'

In his daily round of interviews, debates and broadcasts, Pat meets some of the most influential people in the public arena, and he laughs at the memory of when he was a starstruck little boy, staring in awe at the faces of celebrities on the television screen. Now he sees them as they really are – as human as the next person. 'When you're young, the very idea of meeting a politician makes you nervous, and then suddenly you're looking at government ministers who are your contemporaries. When you look at people who you knew when they were back-benchers, you knew what sort of individuals they were and suddenly they're surrounded by the trappings of ministerial rank and you see that it's not the label they carry that's important, but the quality of person that they are.'

Now he too is regarded as an 'Irish celebrity', a label that has both positive and negative impacts on his life and indeed on that of his wife Kathy and their young family. 'What I do gives me great satisfaction. I get to meet the movers and shakers in the world. They come here and I tend to bump into them. So I am willing to trade some of my own privacy and my own anonymity for the good things about the job. It comes with the territory, and if it became onerous I would have to think about giving it up.'

When he does manage to salvage some personal time, Pat enjoys nothing better than indulging in a gruelling game of squash or walking his dogs up Killiney Hill or on the nearby beach.

Professionally, life could have been very different had Pat's first experience as an employee when he was a young lad been a bit more successful, as he recalls. 'I worked in a photographic laboratory, processing black and white photos. And one day the factory's inspector came along and quizzed me about my age, and as I was a very truthful young lad I told him I was thirteen – and *out!* I was fired on the spot!'

Although fuelled by his obvious fascination with the media, he does admit to momentary feelings of self-doubt and apprehension in the pursuit of his career, stating that 'a broadcaster was a special brand of person, a kind of person with a different voice, a different talent. I didn't think it was possible.'

Seán Lemass

Political Leader

Undoubtedly one of the most popular of Irish politicians, Seán Francis Lemass was born in Ballybrack, Co Dublin, on 15 July 1899 and attended the Christian Brothers O'Connell School. From a young age, he was a supporter of the Irish Parliamentary Party, joining the Irish Volunteers in his early teens. He got involved in the 1916 Easter Rising and fought in the GPO, though because of his age he escaped deportation and returned to a somewhat more 'normal' life, resuming his schooling and working in his father's draper's shop.

His involvement in the War of Independence of 1919–21 led to his arrest and subsequent incarceration. His time in prison was not wasted, however, as he engaged himself in studying economics and history in preparation for a career in politics on his release.

His big break came in 1932 with his appointment as Minister for Industry and Commerce in the very first Fianna Fáil government, headed by Eamon de Valera. During the next twenty-five years he remained an integral part of the government, taking up responsible posts as Minister for Supplies during World War II and Tánaiste in 1945.

Lemass was keen to develop Ireland's industrial potential and was instrumental in the formation of Bord na Móna, Aer Lingus and Irish Shipping – three major state companies that brought vast employment and financial prosperity to a relatively small country.

He succeeded de Valera as Taoiseach in 1959, and was the first Irish premier to be invited to Stormont, where he met with the Prime Minister of Northern Ireland, Captain Terence O'Neill, in 1965. This saw the birth of a new direction for North-South relations.

The recipient of many honorary degrees and decorations, Seán Lemass resigned as Taoiseach in 1966. He died in his beloved Dublin in 1971.

Phil Lynott
Musician

As Irish musical legends go, there are few as influential as Phil Lynott, who gave new meaning to the term rock 'n' roll. Although he was born in Birmingham, Phil was actually raised in Crumlin's Leighlin Road, the illegitimate son of a black father and a young Irish mother, and received his early education courtesy of the Christian Brothers. It was here that his musical creativity and gift for the guitar were first recognised and nurtured, leading to The Black Angels' Band, Skid Row, and the Orphanage, before the wonder of Thin Lizzy, featuring Eric Bell (guitar), Brian Downey (drums), Eric Wrixon (keyboard) and Philip Lynott on bass and vocals. Released on the Parlophone label on 31 July 1970, 'The Farmer' was Thin Lizzy's first record.

Tall and laid back, Phil Lynott exuded a vibrant attitude with regard to both his musical compositions and his daring dress. By the end of 1970, Thin Lizzy had been signed by Decca Records and their first album, *Thin Lizzy*, was released in 1971. Their second album, *Shades of a Blue Orphanage*, was released in March 1972, the same year the group embarked on a tour round Europe. By late 1972, the band's talents had been noticed and they were chosen as support band to Slade. Their third album, *Vagabonds of the Western World*, was released in September 1973. More hits were to follow, including: 'Whiskey in The Jar' (1973), 'The Boys are Back in Town' (1976), 'Don't Believe a Word' (1977), 'Dancing In The Moonlight' (1977) and 'Waiting for an Alibi' (1979).

Despite his hectic schedule, Lynott managed to find time for romance and on Valentine's Day 1980 he married an English woman, Caroline Crowther, daughter of British TV personality Leslie Crowther and mother of his 14-month old daughter, Sarah. They lived in Howth.

The 1980s were a turbulent period for Lynott with the gradual unravelling of his beloved band. The album *Chinatown* was released in 1980, but although they achieved a hit single with 'Killer on the Loose', overall the record was disappointing. In 1981 came the compilation album, *The Adventures of Thin Lizzy*, which was much more impressive and went gold in the UK. *Renegade* followed, but despite such hits as 'Hollywood (Down on Your Luck)', and 'It's Getting Dangerous', it was deemed a commercial failure.

By this stage, Phil was experiencing personal problems, displaying signs of drug dependency and struggling to deal with his marital difficulties, all of which affected his performance in the band. Manager Chris O'Donnell had had enough and left, saying that *Chinatown* was absolute garbage, and when Phil brought in a keyboard player for *Renegade*, that was it for him. As he put it, 'A once brilliant band was turning into a pile of crap before my very eyes.'

Somehow the group hung on together, releasing one last album and embarking on the 'Thunder and Lightning' farewell tour, which ironically featured some of their best music. The tour was originally expected to last just three months, but it lasted a year, taking in the UK, Scandinavia, and Japan. Thin Lizzy's final show was in 1983, in Nuremburg, Germany.

Following the break-up, Lynott formed another band, Grand Slam, in 1984, along with Mark Stanway, Laurence Archer, Robbie Brennan and Doish Nagle. However, the drug habits of Lynott, Nagle and Brennan were to impede any potential success. Mark Stanway recalls that time, describing Lynott's moods as 'unbelievable, almost psychopathic. It was terrible rehearsing with him, because if he was on the gear he'd carry on playing the same thing for two hours. He'd forget the words. He put on weight, and seemed to lose all his pride in his appearance.'

Grand Slam played live shows throughout the year, with their last in December

1984. By this stage Phil's wife Caroline had left with his two young daughters, and Phil was on a rapid downward spiral. On Christmas Day, 1985, he was found unconscious in his house and admitted to Salisbury Hospital. He died on 4 January 1986. The pathologist's report showed that he had developed multiple internal abscesses and blood poisoning, which resulted in kidney, liver, and heart failure.

Catherine McAuley
_____ Religious Foundress

Ironically the foundress of what was to become the largest religious community in the English speaking world, did not really want to become a nun herself, but had little choice if she wanted to do her chosen work, due to the religious politics of Dublin at the time.

Born in Stormanstown House, Glasnevin, Dublin on 29 September 1778, Catherine McAuley's father died when she was just five years of age and her devastated mother quickly lost her faith and her riches. She died when Catherine was in her late teens and she was adopted by William and Catherine Callahan of Coolock House. They were a Quaker couple who loved her dearly but often tried to make her give up what they called her 'Romish practices'.

However the young woman went on to convert them both to Catholicism, and on his death in 1822, William Callahan left her his house and fortune. Whilst living in Coolock she was struck by the poverty and delapidation of the city and decided to take the advice of the local clergy who suggested she build a 'house of mercy'. Using her large inheritance, she bought a site in Lower Baggot Street and in 1827 built a school for poor children and a residence for working and abused women, called the House of Our Blessed Lady of Mercy.

In 1829 she entered the Presentation Convent in George's Hill, Dublin, along with two others, although as an affluent fifty year old, set in her ways, she found the novitiate training challenging and at times difficult. Her Order of Mercy was finally established in 1835, approved by Pope Gregory XVI in March of that year and given final confirmation by him in June 1841, just a few short months before Catherine died on 10 November 1841. She was laid to rest at the convent in Baggot Street and the process for her canonisation has been set in motion.

The order of the Sisters of Mercy became one of the largest religious congregations ever founded, with houses in England, Australia, New Zealand, and America, and it currently has over 23,000 sisters.

Molly Malone

Street Trader

According to legend, Molly was the youngest daughter of Patrick and Colleen Malone, who were fishmongers. She was born and brought up in poverty-stricken Dublin during the seventeenth century.

From an early age she accompanied her mother on her rounds and as soon as she was old enough, got her own wheelbarrow and pushed it through the city's cobbled streets. Dressed in a full-length, full-sleeved, lined chemise, an overshirt and basque of wool, and Spanish zapota shoes, she is remembered for her innocence and her beauty and her carefree happy-go-lucky nature.

By day Molly is reputed to have wheeled her wheelbarrow from the Liberties to Grafton Street, singing along the way. But when darkness fell another side to her character was revealed when, clad in short skirts, fishnet tights and stilettos, she joined the ranks of Dublin's street women who hung around the city centre looking for clients, and leading to one claim that she was 'a prosperous trader who freelanced as a prostitute'.

Unsurprisingly Molly had her fair share of admirers – and one in particular.

Timothy Pendleton was the illegitimate son of an English nobleman and a poor Irish seamstress and survived by busking on the streets of Dublin and on the kindness of passers-by. Every day without fail, Timothy would wait and watch for the girl who set his heart alight and as soon as he spotted her approaching would change from whatever jig he was playing to a violin sonata which he hoped would convey to her in music what he could not bring himself to say in words. These simple gestures did not go unnoticed by the lovely Molly who was equally taken with the handsome stranger.

But sadly the young couple never got a fair chance to explore their relationship. One day Molly did not come by as usual and Timothy was filled with a sense of foreboding. His fears were soon realised as news began to spread of Molly's illness. She had been hit by a raging fever and Father Finnegan of Saint Bart's administered the last rites. As soon as he heard the disturbing news Timothy rushed to be with her but he was too late. Molly had lost her battle.

So strong was the impact of this young girl who died tragically on the brink of womanhood, that following her funeral in the Church of St John, off Fishamble Street, public houses for sixteen miles in each direction were obliged to remain open around the clock.

Timothy was a broken man, tortured with regrets of what might have been. He couldn't eat or sleep and neglected himself, haunted by the sound of her voice singing 'Cockles and mussels, alive, alive, oh!'

Walking the same streets she walked, visiting the same places she visited, became so painful he packed up his meagre belongings and set sail for America. The ship he boarded docked at Portsmouth, New England and he buried his grief by throwing himself into a job in a ship's chandlery. This dedication to his work was duly rewarded when he became a hugely successful merchant with a thriving business.

We are told that one night, consumed by grief, Timothy was visited by Molly in an apparition. She asked him to 'play the music for me, like you did in Dublin'. Shocked and confused he took out his beloved violin and played what later became known as 'The Ballad of Molly Malone' or 'Cockles and Mussels'.

When Dublin celebrated its Millennium in 1988, it was decided to erect a statue of Molly Malone, which now stands proudly at the end of Grafton Street, around the corner from St Andrew's Church where she was baptised. On the 300th anniversary of her death in 1999, June 13th was announced as 'International Molly Malone Day'

Mother Mary Martin
Religious Foundress

The eldest of twelve children, Marie Helena Martin was born in Glenageary, Co Dublin, in April 1892, the daughter of a wealthy Dublin timber merchant. From humble beginnings she was to become the woman responsible for the establishment of a now worldwide religious congregation dedicated to meeting the medical and spiritual needs of the poor, particularly women and children.

As a young girl she attended the Sacred Heart School in Leeson Street and later boarded in Harrogate, England. During World War I she brought her nursing skills to Malta, France and England before returning to Dublin to take up midwifery at Holles Street Hospital.

In 1921 she decided to go to Nigeria to work for Bishop Joseph Shanahan, who himself had been instrumental in founding the Missionary Sisters of the Holy Rosary. Living close to the people at Nsukara she witnessed firsthand the true extent of their suffering and was so moved she felt compelled to gather together a group of women to bring medical aid and comfort into their lives.

At this time the church's teaching refused to allow women in religious orders to engage in obstetrics and surgery and this proved a major obstacle to her plans. It wasn't until 1936 that the law changed under Pope Pius XI. Now free to give these women the help they needed, Marie Martin set about recruiting others who would travel with her to Africa and be a part of this project. She and her sisters sailed for Nigeria, whilst the necessary procedures required to establish a new religious order were being processed in Rome. In 1937 the Medical Missionaries of Mary (MMM) were established in Nigeria.

Marie's health posed problems, however. She contracted a serious form of malaria and was admitted to Port Harcourt Government hospital, where she made her religious profession of vows as a very ill woman. Miraculously she recovered. Seeing her onto the boat sailing for Ireland, her doctor said, 'never let me see that woman in Africa again!'

On the long journey home she recovered her strength and on arrival in Ireland continued her work. The Foundress opened a house of studies at Booterstown and a novitiate at Collon, as well as the congregation's Motherhouse in what used to be the hospital in Drogheda.

Her part in convincing the church to recognise the powerful work that could be done by women in religious orders saw her honoured by both the International Red Cross and the Royal College of Surgeons of Ireland. She died in Drogheda on 27 January 1975.

Today the Medical Missionaries of Mary are active in over sixteen countries, including Angola, Brazil, Ethiopia, Honduras, Kenya, Malawi, Mexico, Nigeria, Rwanda, Tanzania, Uganda and the United States of America (where the order first arrived in 1950). Some four hundred women of nineteen different nationalities continue Mother Mary's legacy, providing nursing and medical care, as well as social work and psychological and pastoral counselling.

Mike Murphy

Broadcaster

As a student, Mike Murphy's performance could hardly be deemed a success. While in Terenure College he admits 'doing very badly'. 'I failed my Inter and then my father tried sending me to Synge Street school, where he had gone, and I only lasted three weeks. I absolutely hated it. It was all walls and concrete and I hated it – I wouldn't take off my Terenure College cap, a fact that, on reflection, probably did little to encourage the art of forming friendships! Everyone was hitting me, the teachers were hitting me, the pupils were hitting me! I went to Coláiste Mhuire, only for three days – I couldn't speak Irish – then back to Terenure College twice, then to a tech in Rathmines, where my father was brought in and told: "Mr Murphy, your son would really be better off starting from scratch. There's no point really!"'

Mike speaks with affection and admiration for his father who worked all available hours to selflessly provide for his family. 'My father owned a garage in Harold's Cross, having worked his way up from an apprentice level,' he recalls. 'It was a great achievement for him to send me to Terenure College. I had two brothers and three sisters so it was a big thing for him to be able to do that – he never had much himself, just the price of a few pints.'

The Murphy family was raised in the Rathgar area – give or take thirteen other places! 'By the time I was fourteen, we'd moved fourteen times, it was unbelievable!' says Mike. 'I've always liked Ranelagh, Terenure, Rathgar,' he says. 'We also lived in Bray, Tramore, Palmerstown Park, but I love Rathgar – only because of the stories I have. We lived near Brighton Square and could play soccer on the road; there wasn't much traffic. It's unthinkable that kids could play football on the road now.'

But were the 'good ol' days' universally 'good'? 'People lived in dire circumstances,' he says, 'Women walked the streets collecting rags. My mother gave them jam jars. The "rare old times" were hard on many people – death, disease, emigration, deprivation and emptiness. These were tough times. There were *Angela's Ashes* times here in Dublin – it wasn't just Limerick.'

Mike Murphy is a household name in Ireland and his success on television and radio stretches back a number of decades. Following spells working in a draper's shop and an oil company, he set about making a name for himself and, following cautious negotiations with RTÉ, was given 'a gigantic break out of the blue' – acting as compère at the National Song Contest. 'This seemed to go well,' he said, and it led to bigger and better things – *Murphy's Micro Quiz*, *Screen Test* and of course *The Live Mike*. 'I suppose the fact that I caught both my mother and my father out – that was some kind of achievement,' he grins, in reference to two classic televised candid camera incidents. In both cases Murphy was in disguise. 'I arrived at my father's garage and looked like a traveller. And I started kicking the cars and asking for a drive and he told me to "eff off" and never recognised me! And with my mother, I called to the hall door dressed as a monk – and I had her singing for the church choir!'

The comic appeal of those expertly choreographed routines held a special place in the hearts of Irish viewers – ranging as they did from his posing as a waxwork figure in the Dublin wax museum and scaring the living daylights out of innocent bystanders to famously succeeding in catching out friend and colleague Gay Byrne in a particularly memorable impersonation of a rowdy French rugby supporter outside Trinity College. A very small number of these humorous episodes did in fact lead to controversial outcomes! 'People objected,' he says now. 'People complained to the guards, people complained to Bord Fáilte, we were nearly taken to court, a guy nearly had a heart attack once.'

Murphy is also a familiar voice to radio listeners and identifies the time when he recognised that changes were imminent. 'Towards the end of *Morning Call* I was so bored, I had run out of clichés. I literally had nothing left to say and I wanted to get out of daytime radio.' Yet he did become involved in one of RTÉ 1's most vibrant programmes for some time. 'I always had an interest in the arts and started *The Arts Show*, which became quite popular – the arts are something that we have all been involved in, whether we like it or not. If you think back you have always been interested in books, films, music – expand it into paintings and sculpture and higher literature and classical music and opera by all means. My approach to *The Arts Show* is that there is a big area in the arts, not a small one.'

While Mike retired as presenter of *The Arts Show*, his run as host of the National Lottery television game show *Winning Streak* came to an end following a period of ill health. But it is remembered with affection. 'I enjoyed that very much,' he reflects. 'People often asked how I could reconcile doing *Winning Streak* with at the same time doing *The Arts Show*, but it was very easy. For me it's two sides of my own personality and I don't have to make excuses to anyone for it. *Winning Streak* is the real Ireland, whether they like it or not!'

Bryan Murray

Actor

Born in Islandbridge, close to Dublin's famous Phoenix Park, in 1949, Bryan Murray was the eldest of three boys in a 'fantastic family' and recalls many happy days as a youngster growing up in the city, in the company of his friends, who attended St Joseph's youth club in Inchicore. Speaking of those happy days, he comments: 'We played football and did drama at the club – those activities kept us all out of trouble!' As his early schooldays gave way to his teenage years, Bryan immersed himself in sport, drama and theatre, becoming an active member of the local debating society prior to expanding his horizons and making a name on the stage.

Although supported by his parents in his acting ambitions, he took the sensible course of gaining some qualifications to fall back on should his dream fail to materialise. 'I trained as an electrician and worked with a guy in Cabra, who was very good to me – he allowed me time off whenever I was going for auditions or performing in plays.' A string of successful performances soon established his reputation. He featured in *The Hostage* with Donal McCann, *The Plough and the Stars*, *Blood Brothers* with Mickey Johnson and *Catchpenny Twist*.

Television too offered him a platform to display his talents. Over the years Murray has starred in *Bread, Montreal, The Year of the French, The Irish RM* and *Strumpet City*. However his role as the evil and disturbed Trevor Jordache in *Brookside* was a major challenge. To viewers he became a much hated and feared individual – manipulative, controlling and abusive, both physically and sexually, towards his wife and teenage daughters. Following a catalogue of abuses and beatings, Trevor met with a grisly – and some would say highly deserved – end when his wife and daughter took revenge and murdered him. 'The role of Trevor Jordache was just a blip on my CV,' he says, 'I only did twenty-two episodes of *Brookside* over a three-month period. But it was a major role.'

Although he has lost his Dublin accent, he still considers himself very much an Irishman and maintains close contacts with the city of his birth, returning 'home' approximately once a month to see his teenage daughter. Having resided both in Dublin and London, Bryan is well qualified to make a fair comparison between the two. He is of the opinion that 'Dublin has lost a great deal of its charm and friendliness'.

When asked who has influenced him most Murray makes a hometown choice. 'The people who ran St Joseph's Club were wonderful,' he says. 'We called them brothers, but they weren't. They were ordinary lay people who worked with the St Vincent de Paul and we were very lucky as kids. They made a real difference – they dedicated five and six nights out of every week to us.' Obviously that dedication paid off.

Christina Noble

Charity Worker

Born into the slums of Dublin in 1944, Christina Noble's upbringing was simply horrific. Her father was a heavy drinker and her mother single-handedly raised Christine and her three siblings until her tragic death, which occurred when Christina was just ten years of age. The little girl's life was thrown into turmoil and she and her siblings were separated and sent to different orphanages. Christina was placed in an institute in the west of Ireland where she was to spend the next four years, during which time she was led to believe that her brothers and sisters were dead. But even worse was to come.

The deeply unhappy teenager ran away from the home and arrived at the

Phoenix Park, where she dug a hole and found temporary shelter. But vulnerable and unprotected she was attacked and gang raped one night. This incident resulted in pregnancy and the subsequent birth of a baby boy, who was given up for adoption against her will.

At eighteen Christina ran away to England to be with her brother and make a fresh start. And for a time it seemed that life would improve. She married and had three children – Helenita, Nicolas and Androula. But the ghosts of her past were never far away and were to resurface at the hands of her husband who emerged into a violent and unfaithful man. She was beaten on a regular basis, had a miscarriage and unsurprisingly suffered a mental breakdown and depression. Ironically it was during this low point in her life (in 1971) that she first dreamed about Vietnam.

Some twenty years later, her desire to bring comfort and aid to the forgotten children of Vietnam became reality when she borrowed the money for an airline ticket and made her way there, where she set up the Christina Noble Children's Foundation. Described as 'An International Partnership of people dedicated to serving children in need of emergency and long-term medical care, nutritional rehabilitation, educational opportunities, vocational training, job placement and the protection of children at risk of economic and sexual exploitation', the foundation works towards maximising the potential of children.

Originally based in Ho Chi Minh City, by 1997 it was also active in Mongolia. After over ten years in operation, Christina and her colleagues have been responsible for the establishment and maintenance of many structured projects in education, healthcare and job placement.

It is abundantly clear that Christina's own harrowing personal experiences have fuelled and guided her energies. In her autobiography, *Bridge Across My Sorrows*, she says that her inspiration has been her own survival of an abusive and appalling childhood. Her mission now is to let children know what it is like to love and be loved.

The Christina Noble Foundation, which receives no funding from the Vietnamese government, is largely dependent on the generosity of those who believe in its cause. But more help and more fundraising are always needed, stresses Christina.

Noble's dedication and commitment to the foundation have been recognised and honoured on numerous occasions, with a string of impressive Awards including the Outstanding and Self-Sacrificing Social Workers Award and the Kuala Lumpur Rotary Charity Foundation. In 1995 she received a Hearts of Gold Award from the

BBC and was nominated for the Conrad Hilton Award for humanitarian work. In 1997 she was named Person of the Year in London. She received a Medal from the Ministry of Labour, Invalids and Social Affairs of Vietnam and was voted one of the twenty most inspiring women in the world, by Harpers and Queen Publishers.

Christina's life is documented in her autobiography *Bridge Across My Sorrows* which was published in 1994. Her follow-up entitled *Mama Tina* was released worldwide in 1999.

David Norris

Politician and Scholar

Born on the Equator, 'in the middle of the Belgian Congo' to an English father and a mother from Laois, 'and that makes me a Dubliner!' laughs Senator David Norris in his delightful Georgian home in North Great George's Street. Just a stone's throw from the James Joyce Museum (situated at number 35) Norris has dedicated much of his life to celebrating the works of this great writer and was actively involved in the establishment of the Museum.

The young David began his life the multicultural way, spending infant years in South Africa and Laois prior to moving to Dublin. A pupil of St Andrews Boarding School ('absolutely abominable'), he later 'escaped and went to a day school in Harcourt Street. It was lovely because the teachers enjoyed teaching and they wanted to communicate a love of their subject – and there was no physical battering of the kids.' This absence of 'battering' was in stark contrast to his earlier school. 'I loathed it,' he states simply, before explaining how the family's financial status was to play a significant role in determining his early direction. David's father went to public school in the UK and through associations with 'a pretty ancient old solicitor in her nineties', his mother invested in a scheme that was to fail dramatically. 'They invested my father's poor few bob in a trust fund – in things like Rhodesian railways, which disappeared. My mother should have been a very wealthy woman but in fact she was pulling the divil by the tail all the time because of these dreadful investments, which should have mushroomed. They should have been tens of thousands more than they were, but they actually managed to drop – they were less than their face value when she died.'

Norris was raised almost single-handedly by his mother, as his father, 'who had a wonderful aggressive business sense', worked abroad most of his life as an engineer and inventor. He died when Norris was just six years of age and to this day, precious memories and recollections of their early relationship are imprinted on his mind. 'People think I have an amazing memory and that I'm a genius, which isn't true at all!' he says quite seriously. 'What happens is that when a child loses a parent early, they go over the recollections of that parent, so that memories that would naturally have faded for a child who kept a parent are constantly refreshed by being revisited.'

He later studied and lectured in English in Trinity College for over thirty years. So was it this college environment which first introduced Norris to Joyce? 'No, no!' he exclaims. 'Thank God Trinity left Joyce completely alone! People push things and say, "You've got to read this book and you've got to listen to this piece of music," and you think "Oh God!" and you get nothing out of it. Someone once told me I should read *100 Years of Solitude* – why the hell should I? I've had fifty years of my own. I don't need somebody else's bloody solitude! I do love Joyce. He created a certain kind of freedom, in a way. Of the things I do write I would be much more impressionistic. I would be closer to someone like Dylan Thomas, but Joyce is so ruthlessly methodical in a lot of ways. I love the humour in Joyce but I don't think I *am* him!'

Arguably Ireland's most famous homosexual, Norris has recently come to the end of a twenty-six year relationship, which he feels in many ways bears an uncanny resemblance to Joyce's relationship with Nora Barnacle. 'I love that idea of fate,' Norris continues. 'The idea that it can play a part in our lives. A chance meeting can mean you're stuck with one person for the next twenty-six years! It happened to Joyce and it happened to me.'

As an influential figure in Irish political life for over thirteen years now, Norris has been involved in many public campaigns at home and abroad, not least for the restoration and preservation of several Georgian houses in Dublin. Other causes close to his heart include the plight of those in East Timor and Tibet, and of course the campaign for equality and rights for gay people. 'They have advanced here quite a lot,' he says, in reference to public attitudes towards the gay community. 'In some places like Latin America, people are savagely beaten and murdered simply because they are gay, and I just think that's dreadful,' he says sadly. 'I go to church every Sunday, but what happens when we die? Nobody really knows; maybe this is all a gigantic nonsensical joke and you have to take that into the equation, and that means that the most unbearably arrogant thing you can do is to take somebody's life or injure their capacity to enjoy life by mutilating or damaging them. I really think we should be much more civilised.'

David's favourite places in Dublin include the Phoenix Park, St Stephen's Green, the Botanic Gardens and Merrion Square – 'a treat we didn't have as children because it was all closed and derelict'. He adds 'and I also love the docks, walking down South Wall, and St Patrick's Cathedral'. Inundated with requests for talks on Joyce, his Senate commitments and literary submissions, it is not surprising that he may not find the time to miss lecturing at Trinity College. 'I still get to ponce around on stage and talk for hours to various audiences, which is even better – and I don't have to attend those awful staff meetings, which oftentimes erupted into psychological, if not physical violence!' Quite.

Seán O'Casey

Playwright

Born in Dublin in 1880, the last of thirteen children of an impoverished Protestant family, Seán O'Casey was raised in the city's tenement flats. As the late nineteenth century drew to a close, the O'Casey family struggled to cope with illness and tragedy – Seán's father and five siblings died during his early childhood.

Confronted with such severe obstacles, in addition to coping with a persistent eye problem, trachoma, which interrupted his education, the young man set about teaching himself to read. Although his circumstances forced him into years of physical hardship in labouring work, he nurtured an unfailing desire to prove himself as a writer and playwright.

He became involved with the Irish Citizen Army but resigned in 1914 in protest against its anti-union attitudes. He became deeply disillusioned and eventually rejected nationalism.

Unable to shake off the desire to succeed in literary circles, Seán continued to write. His first publication, *The Story of Thomas Ashe* (1917), was about a friend in the Citizen Army who died on hunger strike. He submitted plays to the Abbey Theatre, the first three of which were turned down, but in 1923 the Abbey staged *The Shadow of a Gunman*, which was warmly received. O'Casey, now in his mid-forties, had finally made it as a writer. Further recognition followed with *Juno and the Paycock*, which follows the fortunes of a working-class Dublin family.

After finally making his name and a comfortable living from his royalties, O'Casey's writing became more experimental, and he used his theatrical talent to express somewhat controversial political opinions, particularly in the case of *The Plough and the Stars*, staged in 1926. Choosing to ignore the attitude of patriotism and heroism that prevailed at the time, he instead focused on the human-interest aspects of war, the unnecessary deaths and the suffering of the innocent. This provoked a full-scale riot, and caused him to leave Ireland for good. W. B. Yeats initially spoke out in defence of O'Casey, but later grew irritated and disheartened by the content of his work. He conveyed his grievances through persistent protests and insults, cumulating in a bitter lawsuit and a subsequent seven-year estrangement between the two.

In London, O'Casey basked in the adulation of the English, who were clearly more appreciative of his efforts, awarding him the impressive Hawthornden Literary Prize in 1926. Further works included *The Drums of Father Ned*, which served to arouse yet more controversy in Irish circles and further blackened his reputation, *The Silver Tassie* (1929), *Cockadoodle Dandy* (1949) and *Bishop's Bonfire* (1955). He also published no less than six volumes of an autobiography.

O'Casey's personal life wasn't without difficulties either, with the emigrant entering a turbulent union with Irish actress Eileen Carey Reynolds. Despite his wife's philandering, they stayed together and produced three children.

At the age of eighty-four, Seán O'Casey died. A broken-hearted man, he was still mourning the loss of his beloved son Niall, who died from leukaemia at just twenty-one years of age. The Irish exile's grief was evident and eloquently expressed in the depth of his words: 'O God, to think of it. I buried a father when I was a little boy and a son when I was an old, old man.'

Maureen O'Hara

Actress

Blessed with captivating good looks and that famous mane of long, fiery red hair, screen legend Maureen O'Hara surely reigns as one of Dublin city's best-known daughters. Boasting an incredibly successful film career spanning many decades, she will forever be associated with John Wayne, with whom she shared many memorable screen moments, including the 1952 romantic drama *The Quiet Man*, filmed in Cong, Co Mayo.

The second child in a family of six, Maureen was born to Charles and Marguerite Fitzsimons in Ranelagh on 17 August 1920. As a child she was a mischievous tomboy, who exhibited more than a hint of the feistiness that she would later display in many film roles. Predestined to a life on stage and screen, Maureen was heavily influenced by an extrovert mother, herself a natural performer and talented singer and dancer.

At just fourteen years of age the young teenager was already making her mark on the acting circuit, courtesy of the Abbey Theatre School, where actor Charles Laughton first noticed her ability. On his insistence she became Maureen O'Hara and accepted a role in Hitchcock's *Jamaica Inn* in 1939. The film was an instant success, and the nineteen-year-old Dubliner enjoyed her first taste of stardom. Maureen O'Hara made her American film debut playing the part of Esmerelda to Charles Laughton's Quasimodo in RKO's lavish production of *The Hunchback of Notre Dame* (1939).

Starring roles in *Kicking the Moon Around* and *My Irish Molly* followed, and the early forties saw *Dance, Girl, Dance; A Bill of Divorcement; They Met in Argentina; To the Shores of Tripoli; Ten Gentlemen from West Point,* and *Buffalo Bill.* These were among the first films to be shot in technicolour and they fully accentuated her flaming red hair and piercing green eyes, gaining her the title of 'Queen of Technicolour'.

O'Hara's alliance with director John Ford led to the creation of some of her most famous work to date, including *How Green Was My Valley*, which took the Academy Award for Best Picture in 1941 along with five of the ten Oscars for which it was nominated!

But it was in 1950 that O'Hara forged her finest partnership, with the 'Duke', big John Wayne. The pair made five films together, including *Rio Grande* and *McLintock* (1963), but it is for *The Quiet Man* (1952) that they will always be remembered together. The homecoming of Sean Thornton, played by Wayne, and his attempts to woo the independent and feisty Mary Kate Danaher (O'Hara), coupled with the hilarious antics of Barry Fitzgerald, made a heartwarming tale that has never lost its global appeal.

The two stars' on-screen rapport was also apparent in real life and they developed a warm and intimate friendship. Wayne was heard to say at one point 'I prefer the company of men, except for Maureen O'Hara. She's the greatest guy I ever met,' while Maureen, in her later years, said, 'Just before he died, I went to see him, and we'd sit on the waterfront and the boats would pass and hoot to salute him, and his grandchildren would hear a story about this and a story about that, and they'd say "Did you really do that?" and Duke would say, "If your Auntie Maureen says I did, then I guess I really must have".'

Following a lengthy thirty-year break from the world of film and drama, O'Hara made a brief return to the big screen alongside John Candy in *Only the Lonely*, in addition to lesser-known projects such as *The Christmas Box* in 1995 and *Cab to Canada.*

Now in her eighties, the screen goddess is still energetic and full of life.

Away from the glare of the cameras, the role Maureen embraced most was that of wife, mother and grandmother. Married to aviator Charles Blair, she took on an active role in the day-to-day management of her late husband's airline business, Antilles Air Boats in the US Virgin Islands, following his tragic death in a plane crash in 1978.

Today she lives her days quietly, dividing her time between homes in St Croix, New York, Los Angeles and Glengarriff, Co Cork, but she did face the media once again in August 2000 to blow out the candles on her specially designed birthday cake, decorated with scenes from all of her movies.

'Ronald Colman once said to me,' said O'Hara, 'that if you're proud of one of the films you've made, you can consider yourself lucky. Well, I'm proud of more than that and I know that I've been in some movies that'll be played long after I'm dead and gone.'

Charles Stewart Parnell
_____Politician

Charles Stewart Parnell was born in 1846, the son of an affluent Irish father and an American mother. He was sent to England to acquire an education, where he was a rebellious student and had to be moved repeatedly from school to school.

He became MP for Meath in 1875 and joined Isaac Butt's Home Rule Party. He became adept at parliamentary procedures using 'obstructionist' tactics, and after Butt's death in 1879, Parnell became the dominant figure in the party. He led the Irish land reform movement through his presidency of the Land League (1879), where he and his colleagues fought for the three Fs: fair rent, free sale and fixity of tenure. In the Land War of 1879-1882, tenants defied their landlords for the first time and public agitation reached new heights. When the government passed a Coercion Act, Parnell and the other League leaders were arrested in October 1881.

With the people's mentor trapped in prison, public disorder was increasing alarmingly and in May 1882 Parnell was released under the Kilmainham Treaty, a deal that requested an instant end to violence in return for tenant protection.

The implementation of reforms initiated by the 1881 Land Act paved the way for Parnell to pursue a constitutional campaign for home rule, a change of direction marked by the inauguration of the National League in 1882.

In the 1885 general election, a total of 86 nationalist MPs were elected, indicating the degree of influence Parnell held. This result was an important factor in Gladstone's conversion to home rule. Parnell's astonishing ability to communicate with both the ordinary downtrodden folk and the political leaders of the day made him the ideal person to negotiate and the perfect candidate to initiate real and positive change. The first Home Rule Bill, introduced by Gladstone in 1886, failed to pass; the second in 1893 was passed by the House of Commons but defeated by the House of Lords and the third Home Rule Bill was passed in 1912 by the Commons, but never actually took effect due to the outbreak of the First World War. Continuing agitation led to recognition of the Irish Free State with dominion status in 1921. Great Britain maintained ownership of the six counties of Northern Ireland, governed under the fourth Home Rule Bill (1920).

Despite these successes, Charles Stewart Parnell's personal life was to result in his downfall. He had a long-standing affair with Katherine O'Shea (labelled Kitty by the press in later years), despite the fact that she was married, albeit unhappily. Although O'Shea's husband was aware of their relationship, he accepted the situation in the hope of political advancement and a possible share of Kitty's late aunt's fortune. When this failed to materialise he filed for divorce in November 1890, naming Parnell as co-respondent. When it was completed and the dirty linen had been aired in public, Parnell was shunned by Gladstone and the Home Rule Party split.

Defiant to the last, he steadfastly refused to back down and took up the fight again in his home country. Although he remained a man of the people, fierce opposition from the Catholic church was a bitter thorn in his side and his supporters lost three by-elections. Physically exhausted and dismayed with the lack of progress, he died in 1891, with Kitty loyally by his side. They had been married just five months.

Charles Stewart Parnell is buried in Glasnevin cemetery, Dublin.

Geraldine Plunkett
Actress

To the vast majority of Irish people, Geraldine Plunkett will always be known as Mary McDermott-Moran, long-suffering wife of Dick Moran and mother of Biddy in *Glenroe*, Ireland's popular Wicklow-based TV soap, which ended in 2001 after a run of over fourteen years.

Plunkett grew up in Harold's Cross. Although her father died when she was just nine, her mother strove to allow her two daughters to attend a boarding school in Thurles, despite the exorbitant fees of that time, and Geraldine looked forward to it immensely. 'We thought it would be like the children's books and we'd have lots of adventures!' she laughs. For eight years she and her sister spent the majority of their time in this Tipperary town, travelling home to Dublin at the weekends and during the holidays. But despite having spent her formative years in rural surroundings, Geraldine remains very much a 'home bird', and for her that means Dublin. 'Well, I suppose I'd consider settling down anywhere,' she muses, 'but I'd always consider myself a Dubliner.'

As a child of the 1950s, Plunkett has witnessed many changes in the last half-century. 'The whole pace of life was slower and more gradual,' she says, 'and life was much simpler. There were no cars on our street and a taxi would have been a real luxury. We had no fridge, no television. And we made our own entertainment – we listened to the radio and went to the local dances.' She remembers the live bands in the local tennis club or village hall – a far cry from the rap music and blinding lights of today's nightclubs.

One major inspiration for Geraldine was Maureen Potter. 'I have great memories of going to the Gaiety pantomime as a child, with my aunt and uncle,' she says, 'I loved to see Maureen Potter performing with Jimmy O'Dea. She was wonderful and of course later on I was privileged to work with her in *Juno and the Paycock*.'

Despite the pressures of studying scripts and long days rehearsing and performing to packed audiences, Geraldine has somehow achieved the desirable balance between work commitments and family life. She is married to Peadar Lamb and is the mother of seven children, the first of whom was born in the 1960s 'in the middle of the Beatles era'! They live in Glenageary, which offers the perfect balance between fresh air and wide open spaces, and the hustle and bustle of the city.

Sarah Purser
Artist

Sarah Purser was born on 22 March 1848 in Dún Laoghaire (then Kingstown), the daughter of Benjamin Purser and Ann Mallet. They moved to Dungarvan in the 1840s where Benjamin was involved in flour milling. When she turned thirteen Sarah was sent to an expensive Moravian school in Switzerland for two years.

When her father emigrated to America in 1873 after his business failed, Sarah left Dungarvan with her mother to make her living as a painter and settled in Dublin, studying at the Metropolitan School of Art. In the late 1870s she decided to turn professional and travelled to both Italy and Paris where she attended the Academie Julian where by that time there was a separate top floor studio for women. Her sheer determination and commitment to her craft distinguished her from other more privileged Irish artists of her time. After six months she returned to Dublin, but always kept a special place in her heart for Paris and visited there regularly until well into the twentieth century.

On her return to her native land, she quickly gained the respect and admiration of her peers and was well on her was to becoming an established and much sought after artist. She exhibited at the Royal Hibernian Academy and was invited to paint the future Countess Markievicz and her sister Eva Gore-Booth. She organised an exhibition of the paintings of Nathaniel Hone and John B. Yeats. Amongst her visitors was the great Hugh Lane, and this led to a request to paint Douglas Hyde and many others. She also befriended Edward Martyn who was working on a new Roman Catholic Cathedral in Loughrea, Co Galway and wished to include the work of Irish artists. Soon she had opened her own workshop in Upper Pembroke Street Dublin, *An Túr Gloine* (The Tower of Glass).

In 1911 Sarah and her brother John moved into an eighteenth-century mansion beside the Grand Canal, known as Mespil House. Her monthly salon, 'Miss Purser's second Tuesdays', became a favourite meeting place and something of an institution for the city's creative and intellectual community.

Her success as a portraitist brought many benefits and special distinctions. In 1890, she was elected an honorary member of the Royal Hibernian Academy, Dublin (which at that time, did not admit women to full membership.) When the academy eventually changed this rule in 1923, she became the first woman to be admitted as an associate and a member the following year.

In 1924 Sarah established the Friends of the National Collections of Ireland, with the intention of purchasing pictures and to aid Lady Gregory's campaign for the return of Lane's collections to Dublin. Around this time she persuaded her close acquaintance William T. Cosgrave to transform an empty building in Parnell Square into what became the Municipal Gallery of Modern Art, thereby fulfilling Hugh Lane's wish.

Sarah Purser died in Dublin on 7 August 1943.

George Bernard Shaw
Writer

George Bernard Shaw was one of a family of three, born into a poverty-stricken Protestant family in Dublin's Synge Street in July 1856. His mother was an unaffectionate woman who, it is claimed, neglected her children while struggling to cope with her alcoholic husband. She eventually cut her losses and fled to England with her two daughters, but she left behind her husband and son when Shaw was just sixteen.

Despite these unhappy events, Shaw learned to deal with deep feelings of pain and rejection. He lived in Harcourt Street and Dalkey Hill, taking on menial jobs before following his mother and sisters to England four years after they had emigrated.

What he lacked in material possessions, Shaw certainly made up for in his ambition to be a writer. His first four novels failed to impress, however, and he earned paltry amounts of money. He was well aware of his own failings and recognised his weak points, undertaking with vigour the challenge of bettering himself by joining the Fabian Society, an early group of socialist intellectuals, which transformed him from a shy and introverted individual into a confident and strong public speaker. He developed a keen interest in the works of Karl Marx and became a lifelong socialist, lecturer and councillor.

The lure of the pen persisted, and under the influence of playwright Henrik Ibsen, Shaw became a successful and well-respected music and theatre critic. He painstakingly composed his first play *Widower's Houses*, followed by the controversial *Mrs Warren's Profession*, based on society's sexual hypocrisy and the ethics of prostitution. Not surprisingly, the content ruffled a few feathers and raised a few eyebrows. In the late 1800s such drama was looked upon as immoral and outlandish and Shaw irritated the powers that be to the point that they banned the play for ten years, though it was eventually staged in 1902. Nonetheless, the adverse publicity may well have worked to the author's advantage and certainly thrust him into the spotlight. Shaw also fuelled Irish people's anger by complaining of 'a certain flippant, futile derision and belittlement peculiar to Dublin'.

Cautiously venturing forward, Shaw went on to produce *John Bull's Other Island* and the lighthearted musical *The Chocolate Soldier*, before slyly attacking the English class system in *Pygmalion*, which later became the hit musical *My Fair Lady*. This play criticised the intolerant way people are judged by their accents, through the unlikable Professor Higgins who, in a bizarre attempt to force flower girl Eliza Doolittle to speak 'properly', said 'Remember that you are a human being with a soul and the divine gift of articulate speech – don't sit there crooning like a bilious pigeon!'

The 1920s were very successful years for Shaw. His play *Saint Joan* – with Sybil Thorndike in the title role – was a great success in London in 1924. The following year he was awarded the Nobel Prize for Literature.

Despite his gift for writing humorous plays, Shaw longed to be taken seriously and to prove his ability in other ways. He did not sever all ties with his native country and kept up with events in Ireland, particularly politically. Together with W. B. Yeats and fellow exile Seán O'Casey, he co-founded the Irish Academy of Letters in 1932, which followed the passing of the new Censorship Act and incited mixed reactions from all sides.

Somewhat emotionally scarred, Shaw eventually found happiness in his early forties with Irish heiress Charlotte Payne Townshend, although it is claimed their relationship was purely one of emotional joining and not a sexual one. Following her death in 1943, he turned his grief to promiscuity and conducted a series of sexual liaisons for many years until he himself died after a fall at his home in Hertfordshire. His connection with his Irish heritage was never forgotten and he left a generous sum in his will to the National Gallery of Ireland.

Despite his Irish blood, George Bernard Shaw never held any deep desire to live in Ireland permanently, stating: 'One always loves best the country one has conquered – and I have conquered England.'

Bram Stoker
_____Writer

Bram Stoker (full name Abraham) was born at 15 Marino Crescent in Fairview in 1847, the third child of seven. He later resided at 30 Kildare Street. As a student at Trinity College, he excelled in both philosophy and history, and after graduation he decided to follow in his father's footsteps as a civil servant.

He developed a keen interest in both the dramatic arts and writing and chose to combine the two by accepting a role as an unpaid theatre critic for the _Evening Mail._ This valuable experience, coupled with his personal passion for the arts, paid off when his hero, actor Henry Irving, spotted his potential and offered him a job as administrative assistant and manager of a new London theatre. Given the opportunity to work with the man he held in such high esteem, the young Dubliner moved to London. Stoker began writing in earnest around this time, and early works included _The Duties of Clerks of Petty Sessions_, published in 1879. He was perhaps destined to become a writing success, for he married the old flame of another literary legend. Florence Balcombe became his wife in 1878. She had previously been associated with Oscar Wilde.

However, eighteen years were to pass before his greatest work was revealed to the world. In 1897 Stoker introduced to an unsuspecting public a 'gentleman' who would become one of the world's most famous and feared characters. The story of Count Dracula was apparently one of the many tales of coffins and corpses that Stoker had heard from his mother, who had lived through the cholera epidemic. Stoker's classic horror story is based on the real-life Romanian Count Vlad Tepes, also known as Count Dracula. When the Count took the throne of Wallachia in 1456 he took revenge for the killing of his father and brother by the Boyars of Tirgoviste by arresting the Boyar families, impaling some on stakes and forcing the rest to partake in a gruelling fifty-mile trek. He then ordered them to build him a fortress – this proved the final straw and many died in the process. His evil continued – he insisted that many be strangled, blinded, boiled, roasted, decapitated, hanged, burned, hacked, nailed, buried alive and stabbed, and he displayed a likeness for cutting off noses, ears, limbs and sexual organs.

From the legend and from Stoker's own wonderful imagination emerged the vampire who has enthralled and terrified audiences worldwide, both on screen and in print, for over a century. Through innumerable dramatisations and reprints over the years, Bram Stoker's *Dracula* continues to captivate, achieving the perfect balance between fear and excitement.

Following the death of Henry Irving, clearly the biggest influence in his life, Stoker devoted much of his time to writing and he published a total of eighteen novels, in addition to non-fiction works and a number of short stories. None of this work became remotely as popular, however, as the story of the man with the white face, evil eyes, menacing fangs and black cape.

Bram Stoker eventually met a less violent death than his poor fictional characters, passing away at the age of sixty-four after contracting Bright's disease and syphilis. He was survived by his wife and son and today his works are celebrated in Trinity College through the existence of the Bram Stoker Archives Room.

Jonathan Swift
Writer

As far back as the late seventeenth century, Ireland was producing a wonderful array of talented writers, and Jonathan Swift was among the most accomplished. He created a deep and lasting impression on his country and emerged as a somewhat controversial figure, most notably when it came to expressing views on politics and women.

Born in 1667 in Hoey's Court, Dublin, of English parents, the young boy was raised in what could be viewed as a largely unconventional household for its time. He never knew his father, who died before his birth, and his mother returned to the UK, leaving him in the care of his uncle.

He was educated at Kilkenny School and entered Trinity College in 1682, where he was a somewhat rebellious student, with a rare talent for the written word. His tense relationship with the college authorities and an outbreak of political violence resulted in his fleeing to England, where he secured a position as private secretary to diplomat Sir William Temple. He returned to Ireland to take up a position as vicar of Laracor, Co Meath, in 1700. He published *A Tale of a Tub* in 1704, a religious allegory that lampooned Catholicism and dissent.

In 1707 Swift returned to England and became intrigued by English politics. He felt that the policies of the Whig party ran counter to the best interests of the Church of England and he changed his allegiance to the Tories in 1710. He dedicated the rest of his life to writing for their cause.

It was in England that Swift first encountered the lady with whom he would forge one of the strongest and most fated relationships of his life. Esther Johnson, known as Stella, was the inspiration for many of his most passionate pieces of work. Their lifelong intimacy remains shrouded in mystery, even though there are claims that the couple were constantly chaperoned and never left alone together. The strength of their bond was evident in *Journal to Stella*, a series of love letters published following his demise and bearing testament to the depth of their union.

Despite lack of encouragement and criticism from family members, Swift remained loyal to his love of the pen and maintained a deep affection for poetry, combining it with a love of politics and the religious life. In 1713 he was appointed Dean of St Patrick's Cathedral in Dublin, but did not get the English bishopric he had hoped for.

Unimpressed and deeply disillusioned by the standard of Irish life, Swift expressed his anger in stinging attacks against the government of the day and as a result attracted much controversy. During the 1720s he issued several pamphlets advocating a boycott of English goods, and criticising exploitative and absentee landlords.

Swift's best-known work, *Gulliver's Travels*, was created in 1720 and published anonymously in 1726. This fantasy tale of a sailor shipwrecked in the land of Lilliput with six-inch high inhabitants remains a compelling and enchanting world of magic and fun for children everywhere. The travels and adventures of Gulliver were to earn Jonathan Swift substantial royalties, one-third of which he donated towards the establishment of St Patrick's Hospital for Imbeciles, making him one of the first people to recognise mental illness as an actual medical condition and to treat its sufferers with respect. Ironically, he himself was committed to a similar institution following the progression of Menieres disease. He died in 1745. He was laid to rest in St Patrick's Cathedral alongside his beloved Stella, who had died twelve years previously.

A complex yet intriguing character, Jonathan Swift was a man who at times seemed at war with himself while at other times he simply seemed content in his own company. In anticipation of his own death, he penned this epitaph:

Yet malice never was his aim

He lashed the vice but spared the name

No individual could resent

Where thousands equally were meant ...

Matt Talbot

Reformed alcoholic

Born at 13 Aldborough Court, off the North Strand, on 2 May 1856, Matt was the second of twelve children born to Charles and Elizabeth Talbot. He was raised in a working-class family with little financial stability or security. He flitted in and out of school and took his first taste of alcohol at the age of twelve while working in a wine bottling store – a period of his life that set the scene for many years of poverty, despair and alcoholic oblivion.

For the next several years he lived a desolate and miserable existence in a one-room flat at Upper Rutland Street, spending any money he had on alcohol. Somehow he managed to fight back against his addiction and took his first brave steps on the path to Christianity. At twenty-eight years of age he went to confession and 'took the Pledge' to abstain from alcohol for three months. During this time his will was tested to the limit, but his resilience and strength of spirit won through and he remained abstinent for the rest of his life, finding great solace in his faith. He attended Mass daily and embarked on a challenging regime of prayer, fasting and almsgiving. He gave away most of his wages every week to the poor at home and abroad.

Throughout his final years Matt Talbot managed to survive on paltry contributions from the National Health Insurance before declining rapidly, passing away in Granby Lane on his way to daily Mass on 7 June 1925.

Penitential chains were found on his body after his death and by 1931 the first inquiry into his life had begun. In 1952, almost three decades after Matt Talbot's death, the Holy See established the process for his canonisation. His remains were exhumed and he was declared 'Servant of God'. The decree on his virtues was issued on 3 October 1975.

Today the Venerable Matt Talbot's coffin is on view in a shrine in the Church of Our Lady of Lourdes in Sean McDermott Street.

Arthur Wellesley
Duke of Wellington

The Duke of Wellington, Arthur Wellesley, was born at 24 Upper Merrion Street in 1769, the son of the Earl of Mornington and a mother who expressed little affection. As a young boy, he attended Whyte's Academy in Grafton Street, where the famous Bewley's Café now stands, prior to travelling to England to further pursue his schooling. A somewhat introverted teenager, he displayed few social skills and, following completion of his education, he joined the army. This move was aided through the intervention of his older brother and he accepted the role of aide de camp to the lord lieutenant of Ireland while maintaining a seat in the Irish Parliament as MP for Trim in 1790.

The development of Arthur's political inclinations was carefully balanced with his military career and he became heavily involved in the battle with revolutionary France. His seven long years in service saw the gradual development of an admirable record of bravery and vital negotiating skills. Those outstanding qualities did not go unnoticed by the relevant authorities and a series of prestigious titles followed. He was appointed Duke in 1814 and awarded a knighthood. As Commander in Chief of the British army in the Peninsular War, he proved an instrumental force in the subsequent downfall of Napoleon in the Battle of Waterloo, clearly one of the greatest political moments of his life.

Although attracting a substantial level of support in England, a stint as Prime Minister in 1828 was less successful, partly due to his unpredictable behaviour and outspoken views. This fiery combination contributed to his perceived image as an unpopular bureaucratic representative, to the point where he suffered personal and deeply vicious attacks.

The romantic life of the Duke of Wellington proved as psychedelic and abstract as his public life. As a young adult he firmly set his sights on one Catherine Pakenham, daughter of Lord Longford, pursuing her relentlessly for over a decade. However, he later mysteriously changed his mind and made the rather degrading observation: 'She is grown ugly, by Jove!' Despite this ruthless attitude, the couple did in fact marry and had two sons. But this was an afflicted union and one that was deeply regretted, plagued by lengthy separations and infidelity on the part of Arthur, who was known to have strayed with a number of women. One such scorned lady threatened to publicly expose his philandering but he remained unmoved and unaffected by her bitterness, uttering the famed retort: 'Publish and be damned!'

He died in 1852 and is buried alongside Nelson in Westminster Abbey. This final resting place is clearly a far cry from his early Irish ancestry, a part of Wellington persistently played down by the claim that 'if someone is born in a stable, it does not make them a horse!'

In his days in the field, the Duke of Wellington favoured a type of half boot, which became extremely popular and was known as the 'Wellington Boot', the ancestor of today's 'wellies'.

Marty Whelan

Broadcaster

Broadcaster and television presenter Marty Whelan has an unusual sanctuary in which to relax. 'This may be an only child thing,' he reflects, 'but I have a great sense of solace and contemplation in my folks' backyard. Something about being there makes me feel secure in my mind – I enjoy sitting in their back garden, there's a great sense of contentment and security. It's a good feeling.'

Marty Whelan is animated, energetic and very much enjoying his current run of success. Born and raised in Killester, he was a pupil of the nearby Belgrove National School in Clontarf. To this day, the very image of that cosy classroom conjures up vivid memories. 'I was in Miss Walker's class,' he recalls, adding, 'a little school for little people! I still go there sometimes – although it has changed dramatically and a lot of the people are gone, the building is still the same, it looks the same and it smells the same. I still get nervous when I go back!' he laughs.

As a teenager, Marty attended St Paul's in Raheny and, despite being an only child, was never lonely, established strong friendships and grew into a carefree and confident adolescent. 'Unless I was interested in the topic I was doing, I didn't try too hard at school. I did well at English and history but wasn't that good at maths. Sport didn't really appeal to me, but music did.'

Evidently so, for music was to play a significant role in Marty Whelan's life, beginning with those early days of socialising in the Grove, a period described with great fondness. 'The Grove was great. You had a membership card and if you didn't have your card, weren't known or caused any trouble, you were sent off. The DJ was called Cecil – he was there forever before I started going and forever afterwards! It was a brilliant place. It burnt down eventually – I've actually got a piece of it at home – it was very special to us.' The Grove was also where Marty met his wife Maria. 'It was love at first sight for me,' he says bashfully. 'I fancied her for ages.'

Through his work as a DJ and broadcaster, Marty Whelan has been in the public eye for many years. He joined the world of television with a programme called *30 Years of Pop* and he is now established as one half of a successful afternoon television programme, *Open House*, with co-host Mary Kennedy. He has also proved to be a successful and entertaining host of the Rose of Tralee, following Gay Byrne's retirement.

As a professional, Marty has researched, studied and interviewed many different people, and there is one public figure in particular he holds in very high esteem. 'I've always had a lot of time for Garret FitzGerald, I've always liked him. I interviewed him and it was a bit like meeting John Hume – such a thrill, he's a real hero, one in a long line of people I have respected down through the years, people like Martin Luther King, a real and quite special human being.'

Marty has observed the city of his birth with a keen eye. 'I don't think people know each other like they once did, which isn't necessarily a bad thing either. It's nice to be able to wander, but Dublin is not as community-based as it used to be. Communities aren't the same. On my mother's street, for example, younger families have moved in, relationships with the elderly residents who have been there for forty or fifty years suffer.'

Different it may be, but this city is still a place that the successful broadcaster loves. 'It's great place to bring up kids,' says the father of Jessica and Thomas. 'At one stage I had contemplated the UK, and people were in touch with me regarding work, but then I thought about it and knew I was happier here.'

Oscar Wilde

Writer

Oscar Fingal O'Flahertie Wills Wilde was born in Dublin's Westland Row in 1854, the second son of a prominent surgeon, Sir William Wilde and Jane Francesca Elgee. Sir William had three illegitimate daughters prior to marriage, all of whom died young and in tragic circumstances. The young Oscar inherited an immense love for the written word from his mother, who herself was extremely active in literary circles. Wilde shone academically and was an ideal student at Magdalen College, Oxford, becoming the proud recipient of the Newdigate Prize for poetry. In his late twenties, he became a familiar and colourful figure in the public eye and within social circles, attracting conflicting responses to his outspokenness, camp antics and flamboyant choice of attire.

His unique talent was soon widely acknowledged through the publication of *The Happy Prince and Other Tales* (1888), aimed at children, while he revealed a new and defining depth in his theatre work. Although his initial attempts at serious drama – *Salomé, Vera or the Nihilists* and *The Duchess of Padua* – failed to create a lasting impression, he eventually discovered his niche in the early 1890s with *The*

Picture of Dorian Gray, Lady Windermere's Fan, and *An Ideal Husband.* Even further success followed in 1895, in what was to be acknowledged as his funniest and most brilliantly written piece to date, *The Importance of Being Earnest,* which has recently been adapted for the big screen.

Wilde lived the life of a distinguished individual and on one occasion, while travelling abroad, announced to customs officers 'I have nothing to declare except my genius!' Such one-liners were central to the public image of this vibrant personality, a man whose wit endeared him to the hearts and minds of both his peers and future generations.

The playwright's own personal life was rarely lacking in drama. Tormented by strong sexual feelings towards men and confusing emotions, he denied his true self for some time and embarked on a string of dangerous liaisons, before marrying Constance Lloyd in 1884. Wilde remained a man tortured by inner turmoil, confessing to his close friend Frank Harris that his wife's two pregnancies left him 'repelled'. His inner demons were to contribute to his eventual downfall when the father of a close male friend, Lord Alfred Douglas, began a full-scale hate campaign, based on allegations that he was seducing and corrupting his son. This was in the late 1800s, at a time when homosexuality was frowned upon and punishable by law. Wilde suffered greatly at the cruel hands of the instigator of these remarks, the Marquess of Queensberry, to the point where he could literally take no more and, against the better judgement of close friends, felt aggrieved enough to initiate court proceedings for libel. Unfortunately, this quest for justice backfired and he failed to impress the judge with his contribution to the court. In May 1895 he was sentenced to two years in jail for homosexual offences and indecent acts.

Imprisoned, bankrupt, emotionally shattered by the death of his beloved mother, and disillusioned with his lover, Bosie, Wilde became a broken man and only survived this solitary period by escaping into writing. *The Ballad of Reading Gaol* and *De Profundis* reflect two years' hard labour, which took its toll on his health.

On his release he fled to France and spent the remaining three years of his life in a state of poverty and ill health, though retaining that unique sense of humour and wit. It is said that as he lay on his deathbed he stared at the wallpaper and quipped, 'Either it goes or I go.' And he did. Oscar Wilde died in 1900 at the relatively young age of forty-six years, after contracting meningitis. He was laid to rest in Père Lachaise cemetery in Paris.

Peg Woffington
Actress

One of the most outstanding theatrical ladies of her time, Peg (Margaret) Woffington was born in Dublin in 1714, the daughter of a bricklayer and a laundress, and first revealed incredible talent for wooing audiences as a child when she was forced to sing openly in the streets of the city (to support her mother and sister). At just ten years of age she made her theatrical debut playing Polly Peachum in John Gay's *The Beggar's Opera* and on the success of her expanding repertoire, moved to London. She first performed there in the role of Macheath in 1732 and her professional career got off to an impressive start with her portrayal of Ophelia in William Shakespeare's *Hamlet* in 1737.

She clearly dominated the stage at Drury Lane between 1740 and 1746, Dublin between 1747 and 1754, and Covent Garden between 1754 and 1757 and won rave reviews for her role as Sylvia in George Farquhar's *Recruiting Officer* and had a natural flair for comedy, as evident in *Millimant*. But it was for her 'breeches part' – (a male part) Sir Harry Wildair in *The Constant Couple* (written by the Derry-born

George Farquhar) that she was most well known – and it was a role that endeared her to audiences both at home and abroad.

She also starred as Clarissa in Shakespeare's *Rosalind and Mistress Ford* and in 1741 teamed up with David Garrick. She was his leading lady in London and Dublin from 1741-48 and their union, both on and off stage, was well publicised. However their professional relationship encountered difficulties when it became clear that Garrick wanted her to play under his direction and the fiercely independent Peg was having none of it. She was the only female member of the Beefsteak Club and praised for an 'understanding rare in females'.

Graceful, tall and unarguably attractive, Peg had a string of lovestruck admirers and earned a reputation for her many sexual liaisons, particularly her *ménage à trois* with Charles Macklin and Garrick. In truth she is only known to have had four lovers, one of whom was statesman Edmund Burke.

She first fell ill doing what she loved the most – she was taken ill while appearing as Rosalind in *As You Like It* in May 1757. A professional to the last she delivered her line with true determination: 'If I were a woman, I would kiss as many of you as had beards that pleased me,' she said, before staggering off a benefit performance. Perhaps aware of her imminent death she established a pension fund for her mother and sister and endowed almshouses at Teddington on the Thames. She died in 1760.

Charles Reade's play *Masks and Faces* and his novel *Peg Woffington* are based on her life.

Theobald Wolfe Tone
Patriot

Born in Stafford Street in 1763 (which later became Wolfe Tone Street in his honour), Theobald Wolfe Tone was the eldest son of a wealthy Protestant coach manufacturer. Throughout his teenage years he expressed a growing desire to fulfil his ambition of joining the British army, an issue that aroused deep opposition from his father with the result that he somewhat reluctantly took up law studies at Trinity College in the year 1781.

Although he persevered for a full five years, Wolfe Tone emerged as a rebellious and unconventional young man who chose the then sixteen-year-old Matilda Witherington as his bride. Although he himself held no specific religious persuasion, he was sensitive to the views and needs of those who did and played a part in the battle to confront the religious divide which existed in Ireland. He composed and distributed a leaflet on the subject, entitled *An Argument on Behalf of the Catholics of Ireland.*

This desire to succeed was duly noted by the authorities and led to his appointment to the position of Assistant Secretary of the Catholic Committee, a group that dedicated itself to the advancement of Catholic rights. Despite failure in a number of his assignments, Wolfe Tone was duly rewarded for his work and received great recognition – a gold medal and £1,500 for his outstanding level of commitment.

It wasn't long before his resilience and reputation for getting things done earned him a steady and loyal following, not least from the Protestant radicals of Belfast who were a cooperative source in assisting him to establish an organisation named the Society of United Irishmen, a group that made it a priority 'to substitute the common name of Irishmen in place of the denomination of Protestant, Catholic and Dissenter' and 'break the connection with England, the never failing source of all our political evils'. This group was so successful that an additional related branch was opened in Dublin.

In early 1796, Wolfe Tone's political inclinations led him to France, still retaining a desire to see an Irish uprising. The ships he commissioned to take arms and men to Ireland, following many failed attempts, eventually made it into Irish waters in 1798 but were defeated in battle. As soon as he set foot on solid ground, he was recognised and taken to Dublin. He was subsequently tried and sentenced to die by hanging. In spite of pleas for leniency and campaigns by John Philpot Curran, a prominent lawyer at the time, Wolfe Tone's resolve was weakened and his spirit defeated.

On the morning of his scheduled execution he was discovered in his cell with what is believed to have been a self-inflicted throat wound. He died a week later, on 19 November 1798.

William Butler Yeats
Poet and Playwright

Perhaps one of the commonest myths surrounding this renowned poet and dramatist is that he was born in County Sligo, when in fact he was a child of the capital city, born in Sandymount Avenue in 1865 to lawyer John Butler Yeats and Susan Pollexfen, who was a native of Sligo.

Despite being born in Dublin and the family's subsequent move to London in 1867, William and his younger siblings were raised with a great love for the west of Ireland and regularly spent holidays there. It is said he discovered his love for the written word following the discovery of a songbook in his grandparents' home in Sligo.

On his return to Dublin in 1880, Yeats went to the High School in Harcourt Street. Four years later he entered the Metropolitan School of Art and worked on getting published, with gradual success in the form of exposure in the *Dublin University Review*, combined with a relatively secure source of income through journalism.

In 1889 Yeats first encountered the woman who was to haunt his dreams and heart for much of his life – the beautiful and elegant Irish actress Maud Gonne – who inspired him to write some of his most moving works, including 'The Secret Rose' and the staged production *The Countess Cathleen.*

Although the potential for romance never blossomed, Yeats kept a candle burning for Maud and they maintained a close friendship. They shared a love for politics and joined the Irish Republican Brotherhood in 1896.

Having founded the London Irish Literary Society and the National Literary Society, Yeats also co-founded The Irish Literary Theatre, now Dublin's Abbey Theatre, which to this day stages his work. As Director of the Irish National Dramatic Society, he had an active role in drama for well over a decade.

The distraction of his work offered some consolation when he received the devastating news that Maud Gonne, after a long relationship with a Frenchman with whom she had two children, had married a man called John MacBride. This, however, was a doomed union and she acrimoniously divorced MacBride after the birth of their son, Seán MacBride. John MacBride was subsequently executed for his part in the Easter Rising and, following a respectable period of time, Yeats seized his chance and proposed to the woman he was obsessed with. However, he faced rejection yet again, not only by Maud but also by her twenty-three-year-old daughter Iseult whom, bizarrely, he also pursued.

This hunger for love was eventually satisfied with his marriage to a young Englishwoman, Georgie Hyde Lees, who encouraged him in his writing and helped him discover hidden depths in his work. In 1922 Yeats returned to live in Merrion Square in Dublin with his family. Now well recognised as one of the most gifted poets ever to emerge from the Emerald Isle, Yeats was the recipient of worldwide honours, including a Nobel Prize. He died in 1939 at the age of seventy-four on the French Riviera. Initially buried in Roquebrune, his body was later laid to rest in his adopted home of Drumcliffe, Co Sligo, under a headstone bearing his own epitaph:

Cast a cold eye

On life, on death.

Horseman, pass by!

Copyright Acknowledgements

The author and publisher gratefully acknowledge the permission of the following to use material in their copyright:

Barnardos for the photograph of Dr Thomas Barnardo; Camera Press for photographs of Samuel Beckett, Seán O'Casey, George Bernard Shaw and Oscar Wilde; Dublin City Gallery, The Hugh Lane for the portrait of Sarah Purser by Mary Swanzy, with the kind permission of the trustee; Guinness Ireland for the portrait of Arthur Guinness; FM104 for the photograph of Adrian Kennedy; John Hinde Ltd for the photograph of the Molly Malone statue; Hulton Picture Library for the photograph of William Butler Yeats; Inpho for the photograph of Ken Doherty; the *Irish Examiner* for photographs of Bertie Ahern, Brendan Grace, Tony Gregory, Phil Lynott, Christina Noble, Maureen O'Hara, and Geraldine Plunkett; the *Irish Independent* for photographs of Willie Bermingham and Luke Kelly; The Legion of Mary for the photograph of Frank Duff; Lensmen & Assoc for photographs of Eamonn Andrews, Brendan Behan, Christy Brown, and Anthony Clare; Maxwell Photography Ltd for photographs of Maeve Binchy, Ronnie Drew and Tom Hyland; The Medical Missionaries of Mary for the photograph of Mother Mary Martin; John McElroy for the photograph of David Norris; The National Gallery of Ireland for portraits of Robert Emmet, Jonathan Swift, Arthur Wellesley, Peg Woffington, and Theobald Wolfe Tone; The National Photographic Archive for photographs of Molly Allgood, Roger Casement, James Joyce, Charles Stewart Parnell, Bram Stoker and Matt Talbot, courtesy of the National Library of Ireland; PicSell8 Photography for the photograph of Frank Kelly; PREDA for the photograph of Shay Cullen; Reuters for the photograph of Colin Farrell; Mr Rex Roberts for the photograph of the portrait of Barry Fitzgerald by Dermot O'Brien in the Abbey Theatre; RTÉ Stills Library for photographs of Gay Byrne, Ronan Collins, Bryan Dobson, Joe Duffy, Pat Kenny, and Marty Whelan; The Sisters of Mercy for the picture of Catherine McAuley; The Ulster Museum for the portrait of Edward Carson, reproduced with the kind permission of the Trustees of the Museums and Galleries of Northern Ireland.